D1616365

# Hot Licks
# for
# Bluegrass Guitar

by Orrin Star

**OAK PUBLICATIONS**
New York • London • Sydney

*Dedicated to my parents, who brought me here and have always supported my music, with special thanks to Dr. Michelene Federman, who loaned me her home to write in during the day those first few months, and to four players who fanned early flames of flatpicking inspiration: Lew London, Mike Scapp, Larry Maltz, and Rob Hinson.*

Oak Publications has conducted an exhaustive search to locate the composers, publishers, or copyright owners of the compositions in this book. However, in the event that we have inadvertently published a previously copyrighted composition without proper acknowledgement, we advise the copyright owner to contact us so that we may give appropriate credit in future editions.

*PHOTOGRAPHS*

Raeburn Flerlage/*cover*
Rounder Records/*39*
Eric Levenson/*45*
Barbara Batterton/*51*
Stephanie P. Ledgin/*57, 157*
Tom Teepen/*58*
Kari Estrin/*86*
Hank Holland/*94, 127, 163*
Ron Elsis/*121*
L. Satyendra/*128, 165*
Orrin Star/*142*
Joel Last/*145*
Sugar Hill Records/*160*
Mark O'Connor/*168*
Eric Roth/*173*

Book design by Nina Clayton
Cover design by Tim Metevier
Edited by Peter Pickow

Copyright © 1985 Oak Publications,
A Division of Embassy Music Corporation, New York
All Rights Reserved

International Standard Book Number: 0.8256.0291.2

*Exclusive Distributors:*
Music Sales Corporation
24 East 22nd Street, New York, NY 10010 USA
Music Sales Limited
78 Newman Street, London W1P 3LA England
Music Sales Pty. Limited
27 Clarendon Street, Artarmon, Sydney NSW 2064 Australia

Printed in the United States of America by
Vicks Lithograph and Printing Corporation
12/85

# Contents

# Preface

I knew right away when the call came asking me to write this book that we were talking about a major undertaking since licks, though central to the bluegrass enterprise, had yet to be tackled in print. And for two good reasons: The number of licks on any given instrument is huge—if not potentially infinite—and any honest discussion of how licks are actually used inevitably raises notoriously elusive questions such as, "How do you solo?" Truly, licks are the great uncharted frontier on the globe of bluegrass instructional writing.

No longer! After an eighteen month voyage of hard reflection and study I've returned with the maps!

The first chapter is an overview. We get to the bottom of bluegrass licks by tracing them to their source in the primal sounds of bluegrass, and by tracking four model licks through the various phrases in a typical song progression.

Next comes the first of two 'bonanzas' —a catalogue of licks framed by the most common phrases.

Beyond a general bias towards licks that might be considered 'hot,' my goal in this book has been to present a sensible and up-to-date survey of bluegrass guitar licks in general. To this end I have restricted the examples to two main keys (in keeping with flatpicking practice, G and C predominate), avoided the needlessly complex or the bizarre, and made no serious excursions into fetching neighboring idioms (a bebop book this isn't). As a result, I am confident that everyone from the hot-licks fanatic proper to the just-turned-intermediate player will find themselves amply accommodated.

Naturally, I have drawn licks from many different players; equally naturally, the book contains more of my own stylistic thumbprint than anyone else's. Since my style is very mainstream and straightforward (one that might be characterized as Primal Fiddle), I think you're in safe hands.

Though licks are by nature freelance melodic agents, their lives unfold in individual solos, in dialogues with specific songs. In the third chapter we examine this deeper dimension of lick life by taking a specific song and looking solo-making directly in the eye.

Chapter four is dedicated to the proposition that "it is not enough to simply learn a single lick and keep repeating it—to really develop you must explore." Two handy methods are suggested. Five is our bonanza in the key of C. Six is devoted to bluesy licks.

In the seventh chapter we turn to closed licks, i.e. playing up the neck, and offer some new insights into how it is really accomplished. Chapter eight covers special effects: crosspicking, floating, and other techniques that help make hot playing a reality. Our final chapter celebrates the five most influential flat-pickers on the scene today, reviewing their contributions, sampling their licks.

In sum, I'm very glad to have completed what I set out to write from the very start—a comprehensive guide to bluegrass guitar licks, a book for the mind as well as for the fingers.

ORRIN STAR
*Calgary, Alberta*
*April 1984*

# Introduction

Bluegrass lead-guitar—flatpicking—is an acoustic guitar style based on the linear runs of fiddle music. It emerged less than three decades ago in the wake of the discovery that the guitar (long regarded as solely a rhythm instrument) was peculiarly suited to play fiddle lines. While flatpicking has developed impressively in the years since, so that it today includes many uniquely guitar-based sounds and techniques, it will nonetheless always remain a product of the great fiddling heritage on which it was founded. So we begin with a flatpicked fiddle-tune to help introduce these preliminaries.

# June Apple

# Pick Strokes

Picking properly is essential to good flatpicking. The basic method to which all good flatpickers subscribe is to play downstrokes on downbeats, upstrokes on upbeats. In practice this means that you alternate your strokes most of the time (in keeping with the normal flow of eighth notes) but not all of the time (whenever a quarter note, hammeron, pulloff, slide, rest, or other deviation appears, you need to pause momentarily and usually repeat the stroke you launched it with). If you tap your foot up to speed, your pick should follow the down/up motion of your foot whenever it is engaged. Pick-stroke designations have been furnished with many of the examples within to help you stay on track.

*Downstroke:* ⊓ *Upstroke:* ∨

# Anticipation Notes (ANT)

Notice that the first two notes in this version of "June Apple" start just before the first measure and serve as a kind of mini-introduction. Such anticipation notes occur throughout most fiddle tunes and flatpicking solos and they perform a vital connective function. We'll be getting into anticipation notes in a big way in the "Overview" chapter. For now, I invite you to simply observe how they operate in our model fiddle-tune.

# Opening Accents

I've added an accent mark (>) to the first note proper in each half of "June Apple" as a reminder that such opening beats are normally emphasized. Because this opening accent is less pronounced than a normal accent, it does not normally get an accent mark. But remember it just the same.

# A Note on Technique

Play strong. All top bluegrass musicians pick with authority and vigor. So should you.

# Overview

Knowing how to work with bluegrass licks goes hand in hand with knowing the licks themselves. This first chapter is about how to work with them. Though we do cover quite a few individual licks, our main concern here is to provide you with an overview—to teach you a little about fishing before we pull in the nets.

Licks are freelance melodic agents that can be used in a number of different songs. What makes these melodic mercenaries possible is the fact that blue-grass songs are by and large similar to one another—they're based on a handful of standard chord changes and turns of melody. In particular, these common elements are embodied in units of four measures each called *phrases*.

Observe any bluegrass song and you'll notice that each line of lyrics is affiliated with four measures of the chord progression, and that the progression itself naturally divides into these phrases. For example:

| I | I | I | I |
|---|---|---|---|
| Rollin' in my | sweet baby's | arms, | |
| I | I | V | V |
| Rollin' in my | sweet baby's | arms, | Gonna |
| I | I | IV | IV |
| lay round the | shack till the | mail-train comes | back, |
| I | V | I | I |
| Rollin' in my | sweet baby's | arms. | |

Look further and you can see that each phrase has a distinct basic sound which it contributes to any song it appears in. This sound is a product both of the chords in the phrase (which we use to label and identify it) and of the kinds of melody lines that are usually sung with it. For instance, here are six lines from different choruses affiliated with the last phrase above,

| | I | V | I | I |
|---|---|---|---|---|
| | Rollin' in my | sweet baby's | arms. | |
| | Love, oh | love, oh please come | home. | |
| And I | wonder if she | ever thinks of | me. | |
| For | she's the one that | means the world to | me. | |
| | She's my | little Georgia | Rose. | |
| | Laid poor | Jesse in his | grave. | |

If you hum these to yourself, you can hear that all these lines conform to the same basic format. Not only do they share a common rhythm, but they all have similar kinds of melodies and they all end at the top of the third measure with a single-syllable word. Such is the sound and the influence of a phrase.

So phrases are the blueprints of bluegrass. And as such, they are the subtle source behind not only the songs, but the licks as well.

Let's get our hands wet now with a popular real-life chord progression—the one used in such songs as "On and On" and "Jesse James." This progression consists of these four phrases:

I   I   IV   I
I   I   V   V
I   I   IV   I
I   V   I   I

Using these phrases as our framework, and the ever popular key of G as our key, we can begin to think about leads.

# First Phrase:
# G G C G   G G D D
# G G C G   G D G G

Like any typical phrase, this one speaks to us in the dual voices of its higher and lower natures. The higher says, "Give me my sound at large." The lower says, "I need two measures of G, a measure of C, and a measure of G, hold the mayo." These wishes are different but not incompatible; to reconcile them we simply need to pay attention to both. In this overview chapter the lower voice will command most of our attention since it is the more general voice and the one associated with licks *per se.* But the higher voice will be acknowledged as well.

Here are four G licks we could use in the first two measures.

## Model G Licks

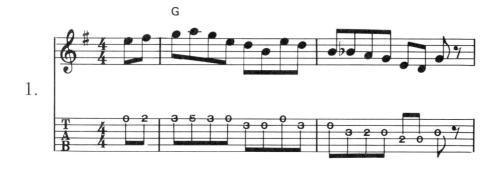

1.

**2.**

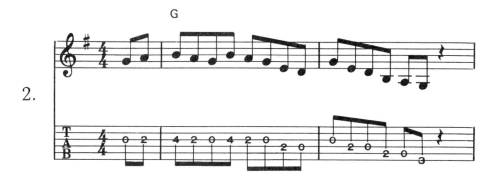

**3.**

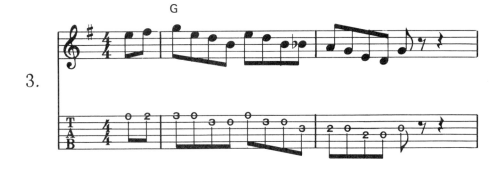

**4.**

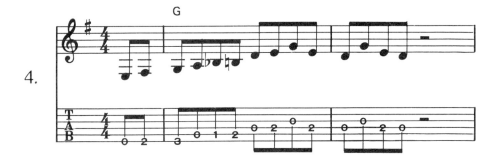

These are typical licks. They each: express a complete idea, start just before the measure with some anticipation notes, end just before the third measure (thus leaving room for its anticipation notes), and generally adhere to the sound of bluegrass guitar leads as pioneered by the fiddle. Located in various places on the fingerboard, and having differing melodic contours, these licks represent a healthy cross section of licks geared around two measures. We will use these four as our model licks, applying them whenever we can in this chapter and observing how they function.

Here are three different kinds of C-to-G licks we might want for the next two measures.

**5.**

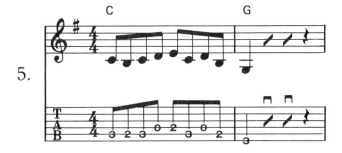

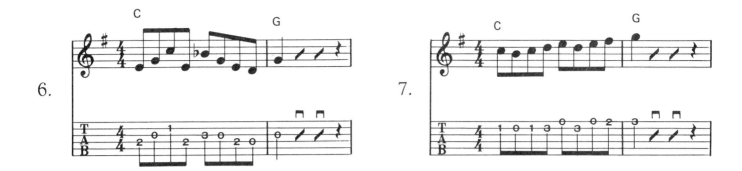

**6.**     **7.**

We can see that the higher voice, the voice of the phrase at large, has intervened here: All of these licks end with strums (indicated in music and tablature by slash marks) because the sound of the phrase indicates a pause during the final measure, and guitarists usually strum or rest at such junctures.

Another thing to keep in mind is that leads are conditioned not only by the particular sound of phrase but by the phrases that border it as well. The phrase we're exploring now, for example, is both the first and third phrase in this progression, but only when it's the first phrase are we completely free to choose the G lick that will open it; when it's the third phrase, the G lick depends on the D lick at the end of the second phrase. We'll follow these environmental details as we proceed.

Let's say we choose the first G lick and the first C-to-G lick to use in this phrase.

**8.**

The question now becomes, "How to join them?" As always, the answer depends on where the first lick ends and the second begins—in this case, an open G separated by a single eighth note from a low C. One option is to simply let the open G ring for an extra beat. Another is to bridge the gap with a suitable new eighth note. Here are three that do the job.

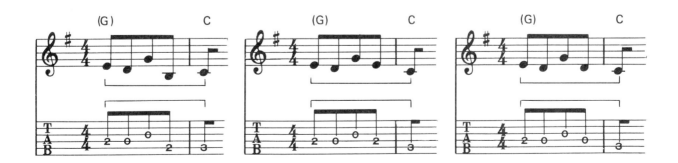

If we were to place our other three model licks in the first measure, we would find a different connective need with each of them since they each end differently from the others. Again, here are three options for each.

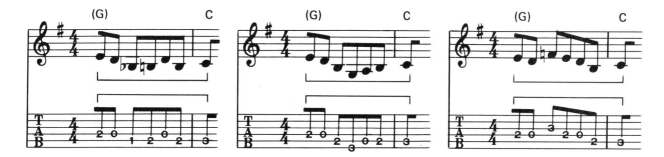

Place a different kind of C-to-G lick in the second measure, and again we'd need to alter the anticipation notes accordingly.

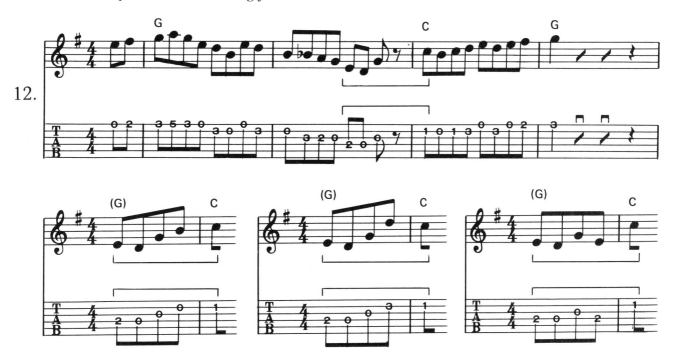

12.

## Etc., etc....

As you can see, these anticipation notes are the key to joining licks together; they are like the notches at the ends of timber logs that make cabin-building feasible. In the examples above we kept changing them to suit the needs of the different licks we used. But they have stable lives of their own. Each set of anticipation notes is in fact a mini-lick that performs a specific connection.

For example, we can alter this recent example

13.

to reveal that the trio of three-note options we used to link these licks can be used to connect *any* lick that ends with open G on the fourth beat of the measure to *any* lick that begins on the low C.

For instance:

Which also goes to show that for each of our model licks there are corresponding kinds of licks that can be employed and connected in the same way. We'll explore this directly now in the second phrase.

# Second Phrase:
# G G C G   *G G D D*
# G G C G   G D G G

This second phrase also starts with two G measures but then moves to D. Since leads for the first phrase usually end with strums (or with a pause), we are again free to employ any kind of G lick we like in the first measure. And again we might describe our task as choosing a G lick and connecting it to a D lick. However, a lead for this particular phrase usually flows directly into the phrase that follows, and so our mission here is broader than it was in the first phrase—we must think beyond a D lick to a D lick that arrives at G. You will see this extension in all of our examples.

Here are our first two model licks (along with two new corresponding G licks) joined to three of the most common kinds of D licks: those that begin on the open D, the middle F♯, and the middle A.

### Our First Model Lick and Two Counterparts with Three Kinds of D Licks

## Our Second Model Lick and Two Counterparts with the Three Kinds of D Licks

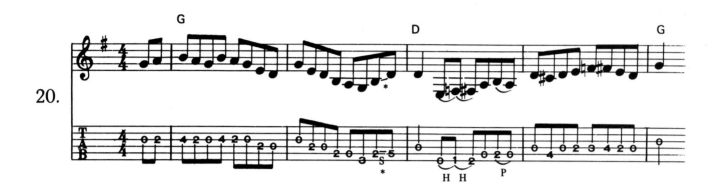

20.

Remember that each lick (and each set of anticipation notes) is a certain *kind* of lick as well as an individual lick, and thus can be used interchangeably with similar kinds of licks.

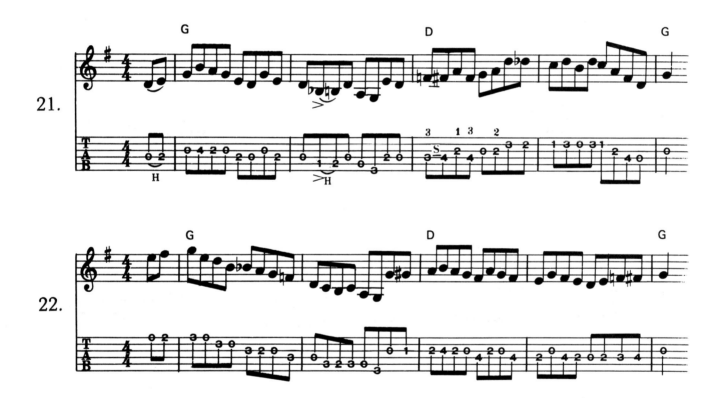

21.

22.

One final thought: Though we've been using phrase-length leads as a showcase for individual licks, all of our examples were fashioned with an eye to the phrase at large. You can hear that each phrase reflects an underlying flow and not simply a random pairing of licks; the higher voice has been calling us.

*You should hold this slide a hair longer than you would a normal one, lifting your finger off the fifth fret only the instant before you pick the open D. Slides like these are common in bluegrass rhythm playing but they make powerful lead tools also. And speaking of rhythm, our D lick here shows that the famous bluegrass G run works nicely in D as well.

# Third Phrase:
## G G C G  G G D D
## *G G C G  G D G G*

This is the first phrase again. Now in the third slot, it finds itself joined to the phrase before it and so the kind of G lick we can use is less freely chosen than it was in the first phrase (or the second for that matter).

There are two ways we can play our hand: We can give the preceding D lick *carte blanche* and start with whatever note it hands us

23.

(which is usually what occurs), or we can think ahead and manipulate the end of the D lick if we have a specific kind of G lick in mind for this measure.

24.

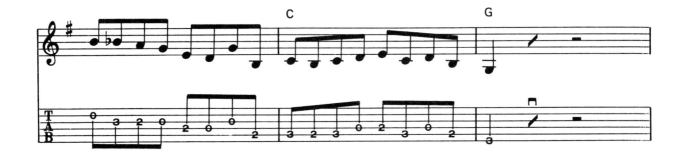

# Fourth Phrase:
# G G C G   G G D D
# G G C G   G D G G

Hundreds of songs end with this phrase and leads for it are the climax of many breaks. As we saw when we compared six song lines affiliated with it earlier in the chapter, the sound of this phrase extends only to the top of the third measure, where it ends with a single word/quarter-note. In present terms this means that the real business of the phrase will be discharged by a G-to-D lick that flows straight to the top of the third measure and then winds down.

**27.**

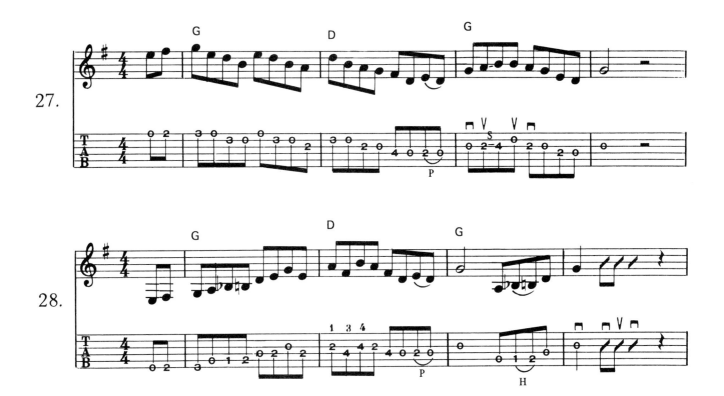

**28.**

Until now we've acknowledged and explored only those licks geared to two measures—some with anticipation notes. Another kind that we've seen (the C-to-G licks in the first/third phrase) but have not discussed are those geared to a single measure. These G-to-D licks invite us to investigate.

Both the G and D components of these licks are short but stable melodic lines that can be used in other combinations and progressions. They employ anticipation notes and relate to their neighbors just like regular dual-measure licks.

**29.**

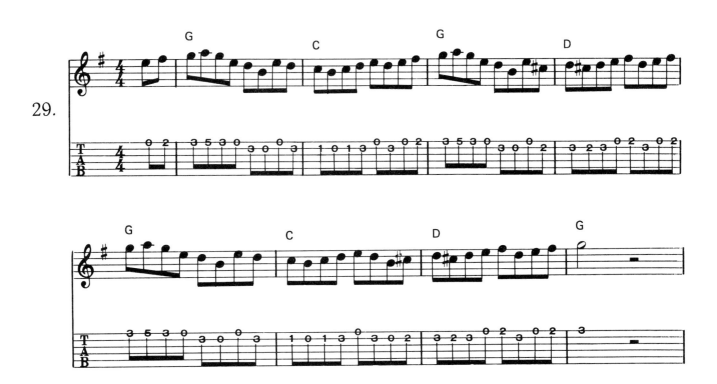

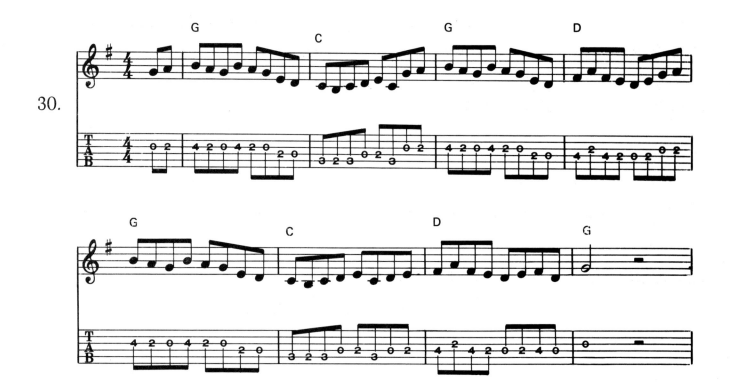

30.

And notice that all our G lines here consist of the first half of our model licks. The fact is that licks are made up of melodic lines, and any portion of these lines may be excerpted and used elsewhere. (The implications of this challenge the whole concept of fixed licks, but since exploring the quantum mechanics of licks is beyond the scope of this book let's continue along as if nothing had occurred.)

This final phrase also beckons us to put our model licks in perspective.

The model licks have told a tale of flexibility: We have watched them appear effortlessly in the opening two measures of each of the phrases in this progression. Yet there have also been a couple places where we couldn't work them in. The G half of the C-to-G measures is one. The final pair of G measures in this fourth phrase is another. In both of these spots the phrase asks for a pause of some kind, but our model licks plainly do not convey such a mood; they would be out of place.

So, mainstream dual-measure licks like our models, though far and away the most flexible type of lick, are not universal. No lick can be all things to all phrases.

# Closing Thoughts

Welcome to the end of the overview. With the ideas of anticipation notes, kinds of licks and phrases now firmly in your grasp, you can appreciate the true nature of licks: choice within order. The leads that you can play are guided and determined by the phrase in which they appear and yet they are fraught with options and choices. The two voices calling together.

# First Bonanza: Key of G

Here now is a bonanza of leads for five classic phrases set in the key of G. Presenting licks within phrases allows us the best of both worlds, for we can treat each lead both as a single unit and as a storehouse of separate licks and anticipation notes. Naturally G licks are the star of this show, but C and D licks contribute solid performances as well.

We'll start by showcasing "opening" G licks as we take a round-robin look at three phrases with practically interchangeable first halves: I I IV I, I I V V (the first two from our overview), and I I IV IV. We'll close by looking at licks for the two all-time important ending phrases: the already familiar I V I I and the brilliant but jaded V V I I.

These leads are loosely organized according to where they start on the fingerboard—moving from treble to bass in each of the three sections—and as to how they sound, so that licks that are similar (or that sound like they'd make good roommates) might adjoin each other. But overall it's a real grab bag.

Happy hunting!

# Round Robin: G G C G, G G D D, and G G C C

31.

**32.**

**33.**

Two new anticipation notes at the start of this one. (They work well with all of the above G licks.)

**34.**

**35.**

**36.**

For G licks like the six that follow you need to bar your index finger across the B and E strings on the third fret and work out of a position that looks like an F chord two frets up. This first one is outstanding.

37.

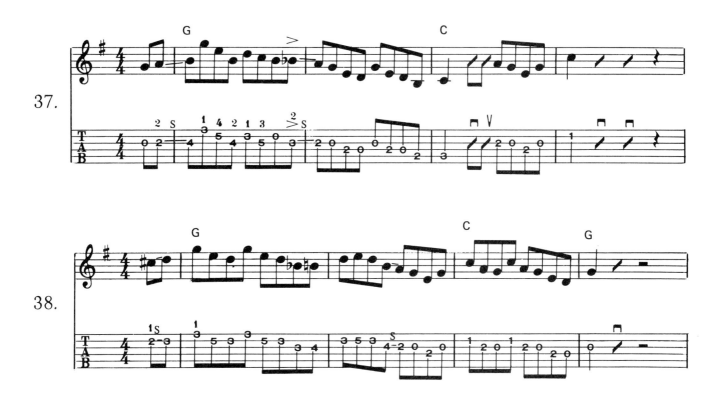

Notice the subtle and pleasing use of the open B at the end of the first measure.

39.

40.

A beautiful C lick here. Let each note ring as long as you can.

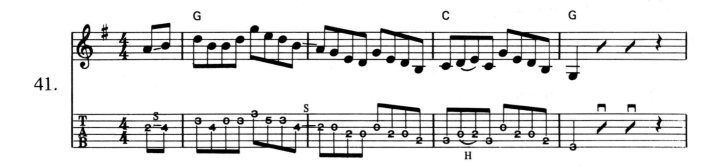

41.

The G lick is from Doc Watson.

42.

A personal favorite:

43.

(Sometimes I like pulling off to the three open Bs instead of picking them.)

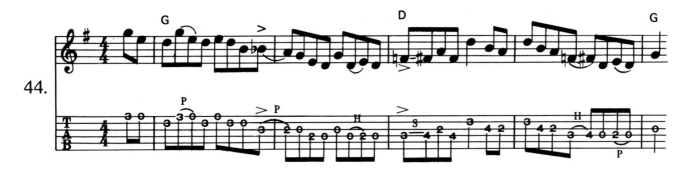

44.

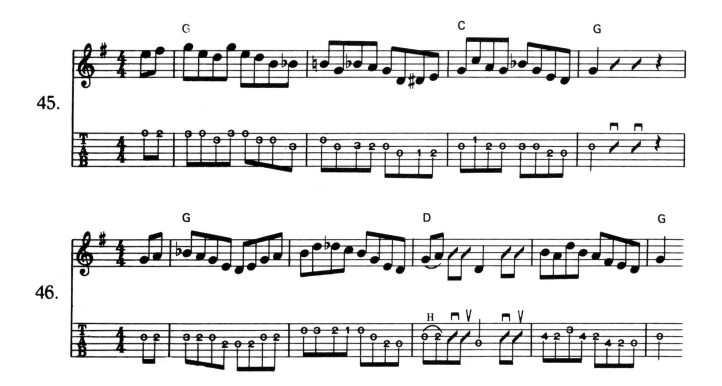

45.

46.

A double-stop slide and other fancy footwork:

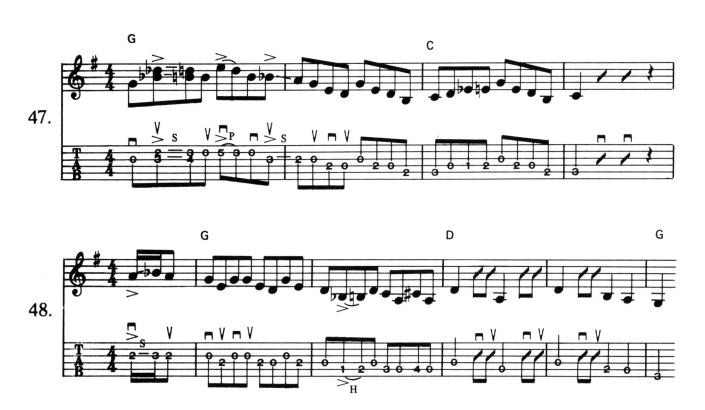

47.

48.

A beautiful bluesy lick from Russ Barenberg (one of the best):

Quite a few of the phrases with C licks in this chapter sound nice when paired up and played as a whole with the D-lick phrases that follow. These next two for example:

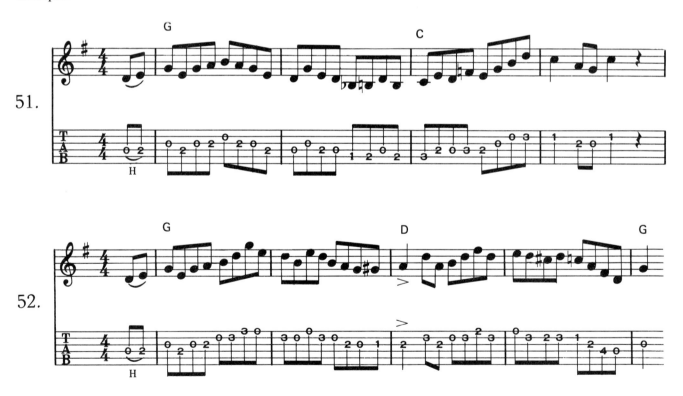

*Twice* two consecutive B notes appear in the G lick. This is allowed.

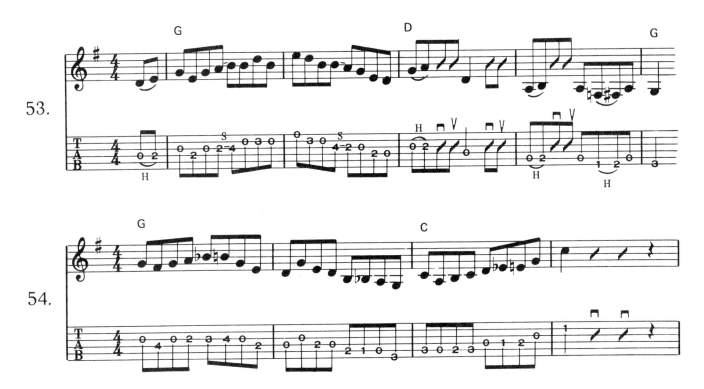

53.

54.

This G lick was played by a fiddler on an early Flatt and Scruggs record. It really embodies the sound of the phrase.

55.

56.

A double-stop rich D lick crowns this lead. The strums in licks like these are really pauses: You must keep them delicate so that they don't compete with the melody notes or call undue attention to open strings which are not part of the chord but which result from the demands of the fingerings (in this instance, the high E). By strumming with finesse you can combine rhythm and lead moves into a pleasing whole (as Norman Blake often demonstrates).

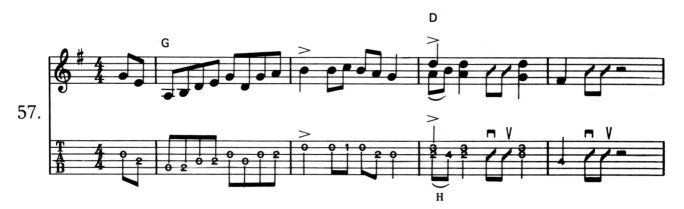

A couple of chromatic leads:

Licks like these can add some real spice to a solo. What's noteworthy about them is that they have departed from a regulation chromatic scale (i.e., one using *every* consecutive note between two points) in small but significant ways so that they sound graceful. They did not come out of the can like this. Indeed, this is the story with all licks based on standard scale patterns—the nicest ones have all been altered slightly to suit the settings in which they appear.

Another from Doc Watson:

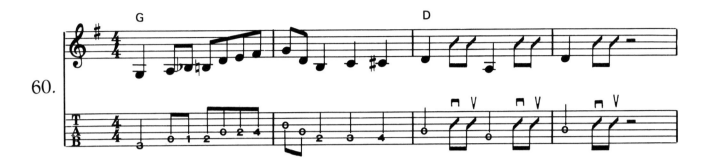

It's so easy to drift into an all-eighth-note mind-set that quarter notes are often the pauses that refresh.

And now that we're refreshed:

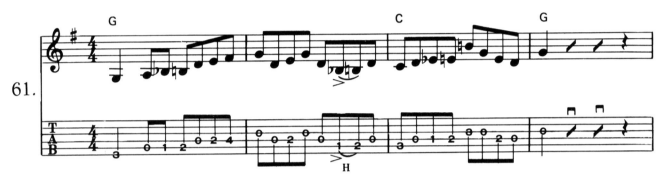

Finally, one of my favorite leads for the G-to-D phrase—a lead so hot that when it was a baby it had an asbestos crib. Like some potent swing licks, the D lick starts by taking each note of the chord and jumping around it in a pattern.

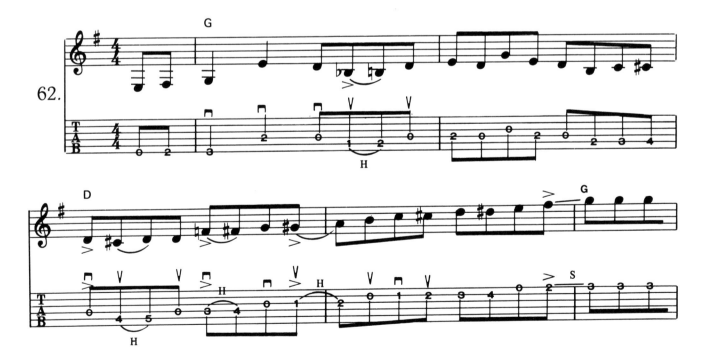

# First Classic Ending Phrase: G D G G

From Doc Watson:

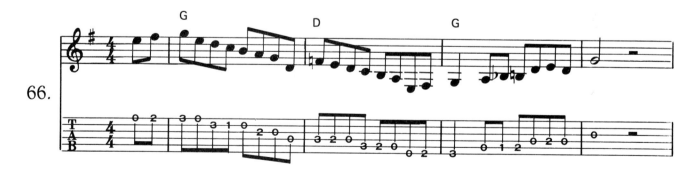

**67.**

**68.**

**69.**

One of the ten I'd take with me to a desert island.

**70.**

This worthy line is from Rick Starkey, a fine flatpicker from Connecticut. Starting as it does right at the top of the measure, you need to count it a little differently than the leads which begin with anticipation notes.

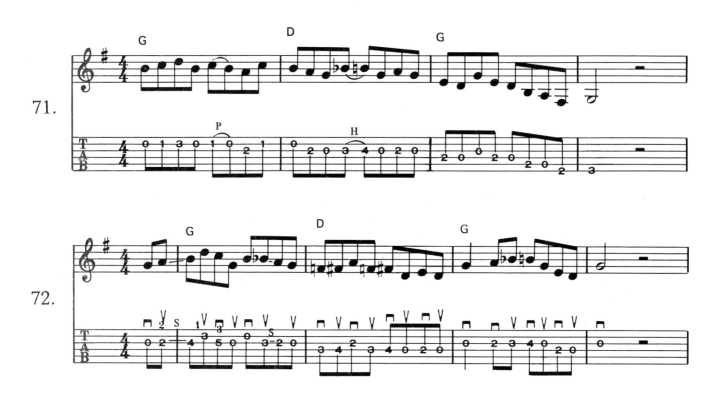

Two from Norman Blake:

**75.**

Banjoesque:

**76.**

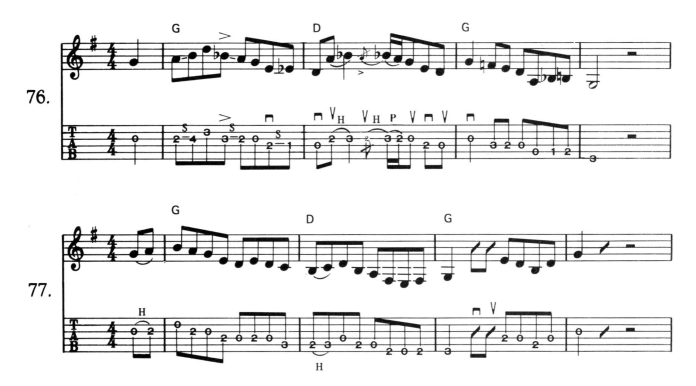

**77.**

**Another from the fiddler on the early Flatt and Scruggs recording:**

**78.**

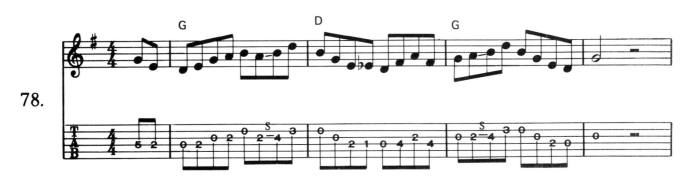

**Leads** like these—which are so unified that they defy separation into compo-
**nent licks**—are beautiful to behold.

Pinkyrobics:

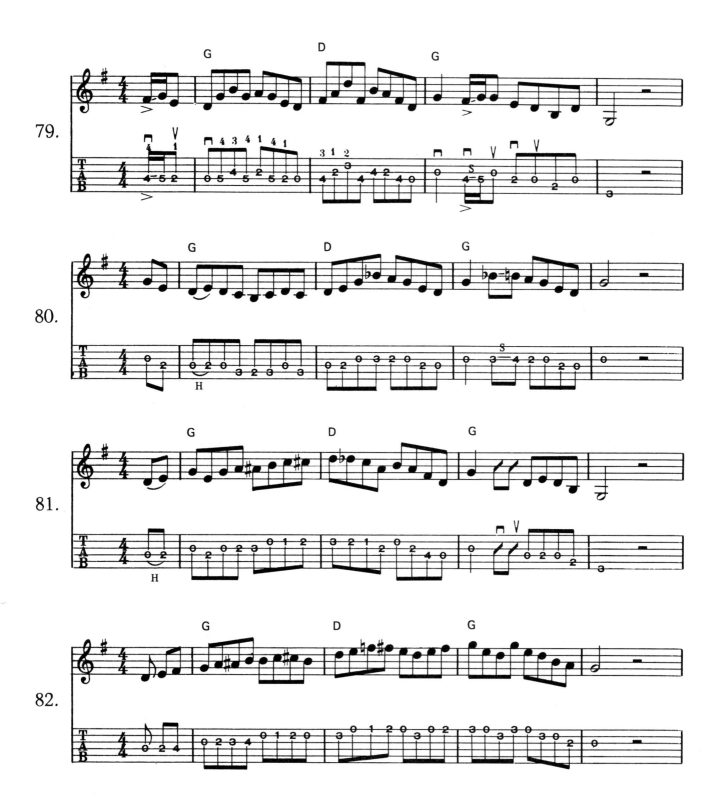

79.

80.

81.

82.

Another from Rick Starkey:

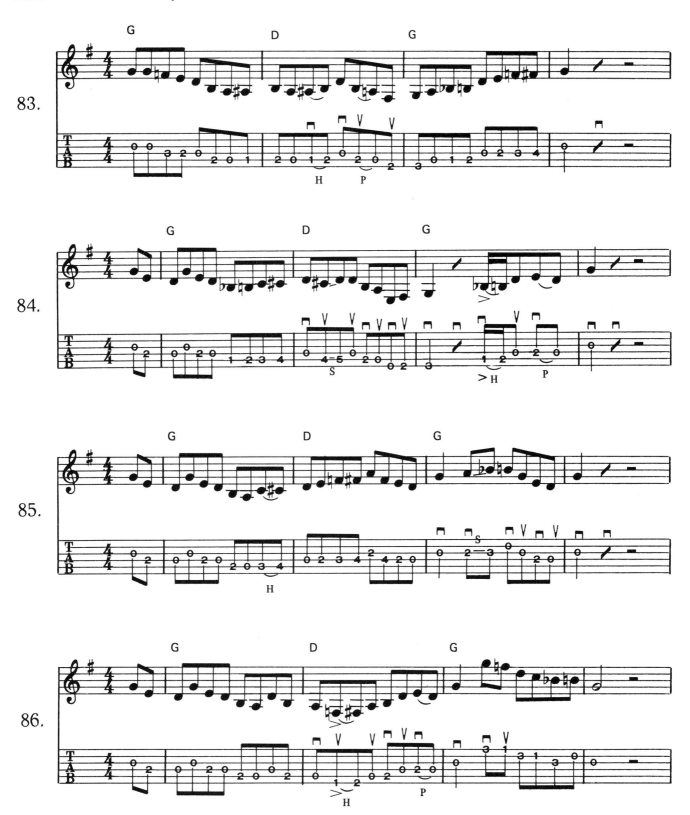

The D lick in this one is an all-purpose measure that works well in many fiddle
tunes (e.g., "Cherokee Shuffle").

87.

88.

Norman Blake rides again:

89.

It's sometimes hard to grasp the timing of licks like these not only because they
start right at the top of the measure but also because we tend to form habits and
to assume that certain notes belong in certain places in the measure. The first
three notes in this lead, for instance, frequently appear two notes earlier in the
measure as the anticipation and first notes of many G licks; if that is our only
association with them in the key of G, then leads like the one above will be a
stretch. Recalibrate.

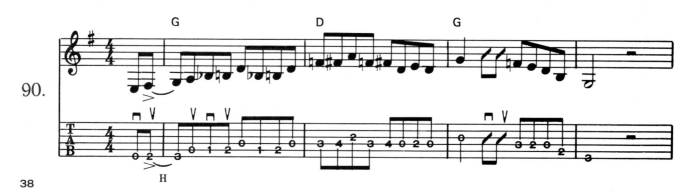

90.

91.

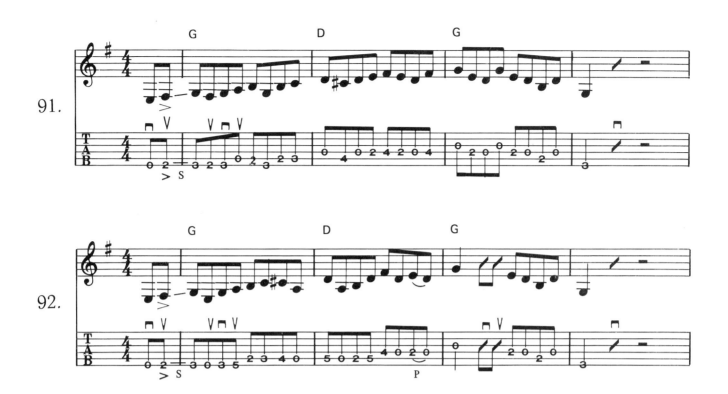

92.

The Rising Fawn String Ensemble: James Bryan, Nancy Blake, and Norman Blake

# Second Classic Ending Phrase: D D G G

The D licks which fill these opening measures are not just any D licks—they are D licks formulated with this G-based phrase in mind. So here they are in this bonanza. Also, I'm happy to report that the fingerings for most of these leads turned out to be particularly satisfying ones.

97.

98.

99.

100.

101.

41

102.

Another one that starts at the top of the measure—so make that first down-stroke a keeper.

103.

104.

105.

106.

**Two from Clarence White.** Like many of the licks in this book, how "hot" they **sound depends** on how fast they are played.

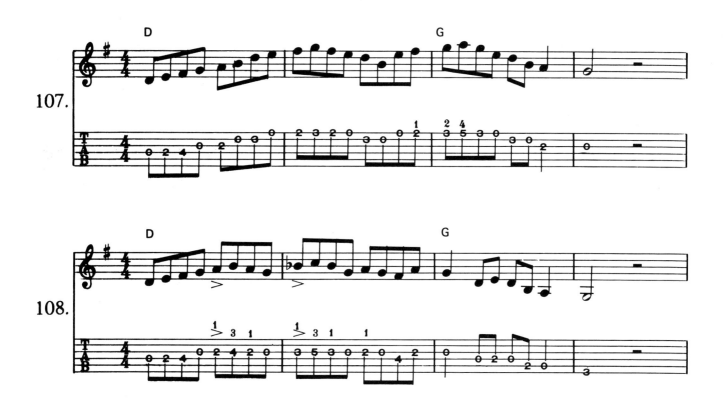

107.

108.

**One with demonstrated leadership qualities:**

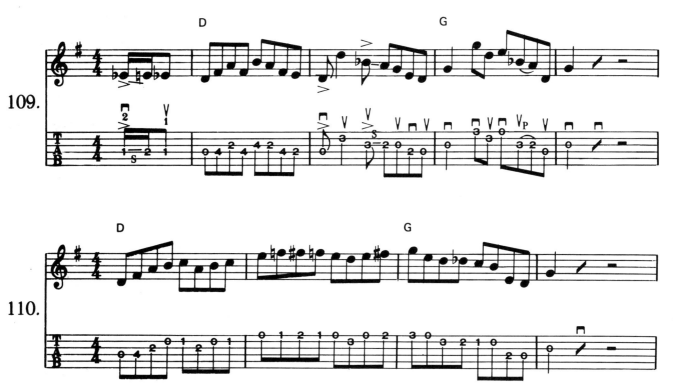

109.

110.

Here are two exquisite leads from Gary Mehalick, my performing partner since
1976. Both start at the top of the measure and feature interesting syncopations.

Here's one from Jimmy Haley (whose lead playing helps verify the *quick* in
Quicksilver) that starts with a neat hammer-into-slide triplet.

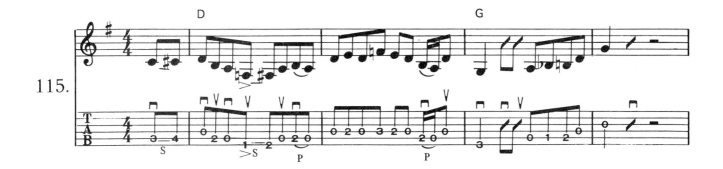

115.

And out with a bang (if you give the pulloff the power it deserves):

116.

Orrin Star and Gary Mehalick at the Corinth Bluegrass Festival, July 1978

# A Specific Song: "Don't Let Your Deal Go Down"

Phrases take licks as far as licks can go without getting into a specific song. But licks ultimately belong to a solo, as parts of a dialogue with a specific song. So let's shift gears for a chapter and consider a specific song.

"Don't Let Your Deal Go Down" is a bluegrass favorite with a fun, ragtime-flavored progression of four chords repeated twice. I like playing it out of a C chord, and so the progression would be

A A D D G G C C

In terms of phrases this would be

‖: VI │ VI │ II │ II │ V │ V │ I │ I :‖

But now we have more than phrases to guide us; we have a real live melody:

## Don't Let Your Deal Go Down

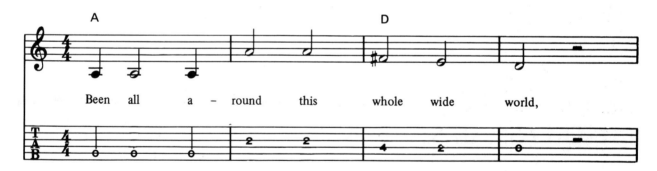

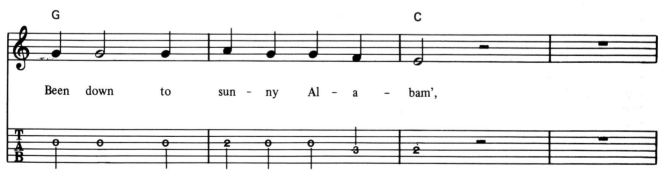

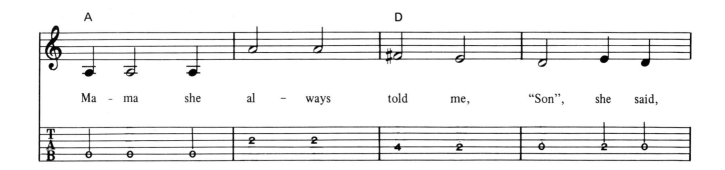

Ma - ma she al - ways told me, "Son", she said,

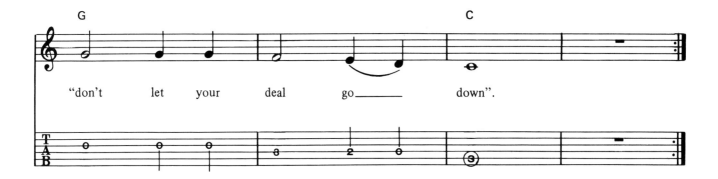

"don't let your deal go_____ down".

A melody is just that—a guide. It is a coherent melodic line running through a set of chords. Whether we follow it closely or only echo it faintly in a given solo, it is our unchanging point of reference. Indeed as I see it there are only two basic approaches to soloing: playing a melody directly and playing a melody indirectly.

We'll spend most of our time here on the direct approach since we already know quite a bit about the indirect from phrases (which never represent only one specific melody).

# Playing the Melody Directly

Making a solo that follows a melody directly might appear to be simple— wouldn't you just play the melody?

Not necessarily. If you were playing a fiddle tune, then it would sound fine to simply play the melody since fiddle tunes use a lot of eighth notes and eighth notes are the flatpicker's favored medium of exchange. But a song melody, on the other hand, is usually based on quarter notes and includes some sizeable rests; if you simply played it on the guitar it would sound dull.

"Don't Let Your Deal Go Down" has a typical song melody and so we must add to it if we are to make a decent flatpicking solo. By starting with some simple solos and working our way up we can observe how this process of addition operates.

Let's begin with a sturdy Carter-style solo.

117.

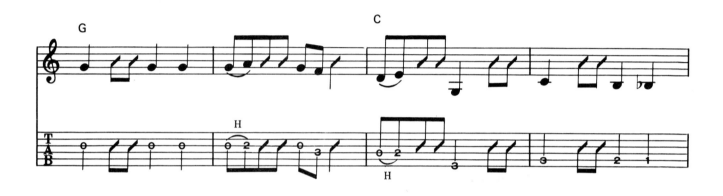

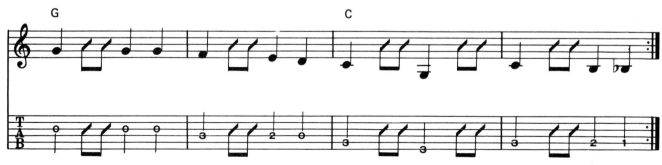

By punctuating the many quarter notes with strums and by adding a few bass notes we have produced a viable solo which preserves the melody while avoiding the highest drabness rating.

Where did the notes we added come from? Most came from the way a singer would sing "Don't Let Your Deal Go Down." Song melodies are not as cut and dried as we think. What we call the melody is often actually one of several possible variations. Even before individual singers interpret a melody, there are inherent variations in most songs. If you look closely you can see that the melody usually varies slightly from verse to verse depending on the number of syllables in the lyrics. For instance, what we have accepted as the melody of "Don't Let Your Deal Go Down" is in fact a product of the particular verse above. If we look at a verse which contains more syllables, we find that there are some additional melody notes available to us.

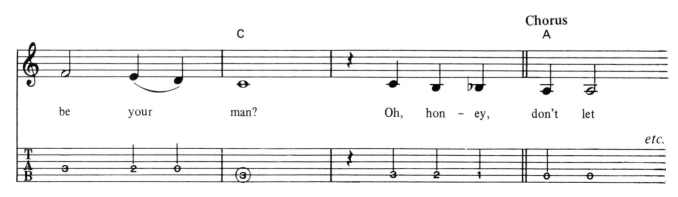

For a musician looking to elaborate or augment a melody these syllable-based variations are the logical first stop. And this is where the melodic additions to our solo came from. (The other additions were rhythmic and obvious; the bass notes from a C chord, on which to hang some strums in the C measures.)

Although our Carter-style solo is rather simple-sounding and offers none of the sparkling runs that are the lifeblood of flatpicking (and which provoke threats of digital mutilation from audience members), it does provide us with an important rhythm-charged reflection of the melody—one which we can draw on in more sophisticated solos. But to achieve some dazzle we must add more notes.

Here's a solo that takes this to heart, subdividing many of the half notes from the melody into simpatico pairs of quarter notes (yet dispensing with strums).

118.

**Maybelle Carter in 1973**

As this solo shows, we can do more than simply follow the extra syllables which appear in some verses in order to expand a song's melody—we can add some "syllables" of our own.

We each have a basic melodic sense that is there to guide us if we only ask. This melodic sense is reflected almost effortlessly in most people's singing but emerges only over time in their playing. Yet it is always there. Whenever we add notes to a melody we are in constant consultation with it, asking "Does this note enhance the melody?" (when we're at our best) or "Will the melody get angry if I use a triplet here?" (when we haven't had our Sanka). Behind the outward skill of the mature player lies a solid connection with this inner resource.

The solo above reflects a connection that is still developing. It is a rather mechanical creation. Though it has its moments (the final G measures stand out), it doesn't express the melody with anything approaching vocal-like subtlety. But—like the solo before it—it is a beacon on the road to the better.

My kind of direct melody break:

119.

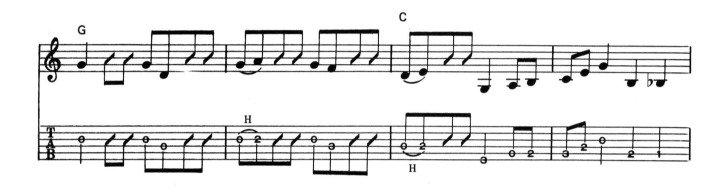

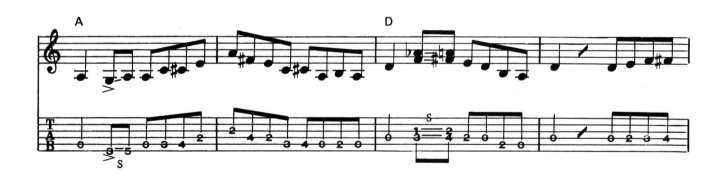

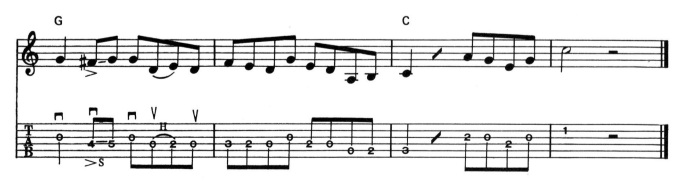

Mighty fine. Here we finally see melody and action blended in a way that approaches vocal subtlety.

Notice how both notes *and* techniques are employed as vehicles of expression. Strums, slides, pulloffs, double-stops—all have been drafted for the cause.

Two points of special interest:

1. The C Measures

    The melody rests for most of the C measures. As we know from our experience with phrases, whenever such a pause occurs we can be mellow and strum, or active and throw in a lick. In the two earlier solos we were mellow; this time we got active.

    All bluegrass songs contain rests like this. They are often coveted lick locales because, free from the example of the melody, they invite relatively pure licks. (Relative because you're not entirely free: The licks you use need to complement the melody if they're to be welcome guests. Still, there is ample room for invention. The two we used are on the discreet side.)

2. All of the lines in this solo were spawned from the melody and fit it like tailored garments. Are they licks?

"Can they be used elsewhere?" is the important question. Whereas licks are by nature moveable, lines created around specific melodies sometimes make sense only in their original contexts, depending on the portion of the melody they represent and on how literally they represent it. For example, consider the lines played against the two A chords.

Given the fact that the portion of melody they cover is not a particularly common one, they are not automatically licks. The rather literal first line, with its strums in the middle, is clearly the more limited of the two; it is hard to imagine where else it might be used. But the more impressionistic second line, with its all-eighth-note construction, is less committed to the melody and hence much more potentially mobile: It is a generic lick and a tailored lick at the same time. Without too much thought we could find gainful employment for it elsewhere—in a B part to "Bonaparte's Retreat" for example.

Going one step further, consider the line in the final G measures.

Since the portion of melody it covers is quite common (popular phrase at work) and it is loosely tailored to boot, it can be used with many, many songs; it is a generic lick par excellence. It works beautifully, for example, in "Bully of the Town" and "New River Train." Our lick in the last third of both those songs:

*New River Train*

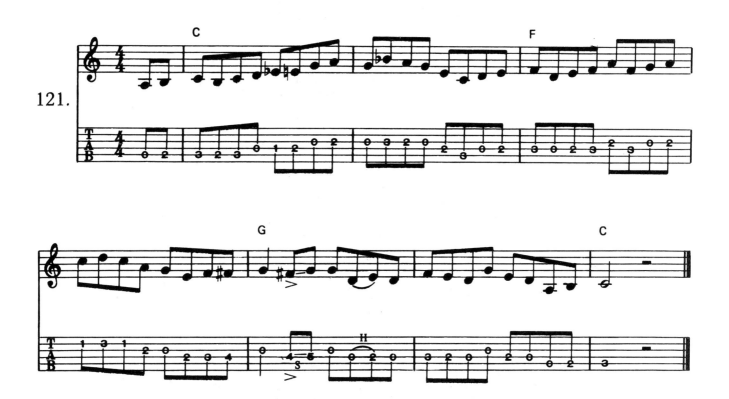

121.

*Bully of the Town*

122.

So, you can cull some great licks from your direct melody solos. And, as we have seen, even pure licks play a role in them.

# Playing the Melody Indirectly

Once a player has clearly stated a melody, he usually refers to it less directly in the solos that follow. His focus shifts from the specific task of presenting the melody outright to the more open-ended challenge of somehow *reflecting* it. He thinks more impressionistically and he begins using licks in earnest.

My favorite indirect solo for "Don't Let Your Deal Go Down":

123.

As you can hear, the melody is still the guest of honor at this party. But it is now a subtler, behind-the-scenes presence. And you yourself are both caterer and host. Like leads for phrases, themselves also one step removed from a specific melody and hence also indirect, the key to such solos is one's own melodic sense.

In the next chapter we'll look at some specific ways to commune with your melodic sense; for now, all that needs to be added are these words of indirect-approach advice: Beware of combo platters offering tempting but unrelated fare.

# And So

We've explored solos for a specific song in this chapter in order to broaden your perspective on licks. You now know not only that there is life after phrases, in the form of specific solos, but that there is life before them as well, in the form of each individual's melodic sense.

The New Grass Revival's Pat Flynn at the
Lone Star Cafe in New York City, August 1983

The Lonesome Ramblers' Larry Sparks obliges a young bluegrass fan

# Exploring: "Don't Let Your Deal Go Down" Continued

Working with licks is like speaking a language. You can get by once you know the basic terms. But the richer your vocabulary, the more interesting your talk will be. It is not enough to simply learn a single lick and keep repeating it—to really develop you must explore. We'll now look at two good ways of doing this.

# Other Octaves and Keys

Try a lick in other octaves and keys. Is it awkward to finger or does it just not sound as good in some locations? Try changing a note or two. Play around with it until you get something you like. Often you'll arrive at a facsimile that's more pleasing than the original.

A great way to explore is to try making a whole break for a song using a single lick. This not only provides you with a structure, but it has the added virtue of requiring you to link the licks together coherently, which is how licks are used in the real world.

Continuing with "Don't Let Your Deal Go Down" as our framework, here are three two-measure licks in A.

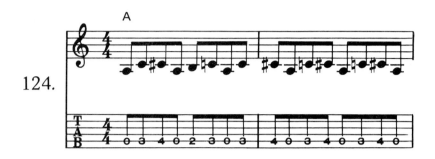

124.

125.

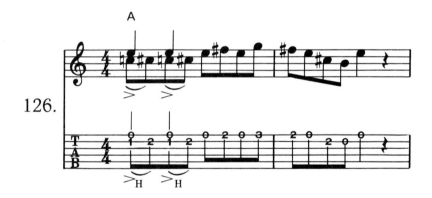

126.

Let's take each one now and apply it to the whole progression.

127.

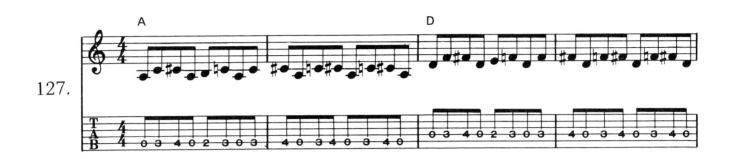

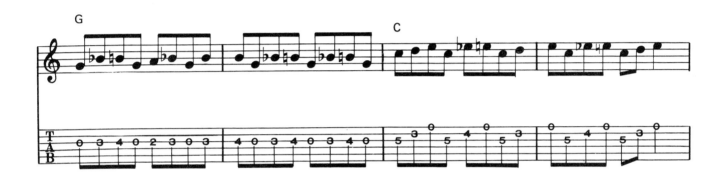

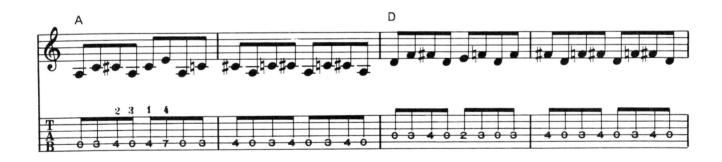

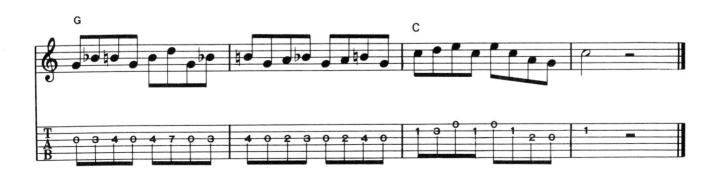

Our first lick moves easily since there are open strings that correspond to each chord in the progression. I've introduced some variations in the second half of the break. Notice how the later G measures set up the coming C note better than the earlier ones.

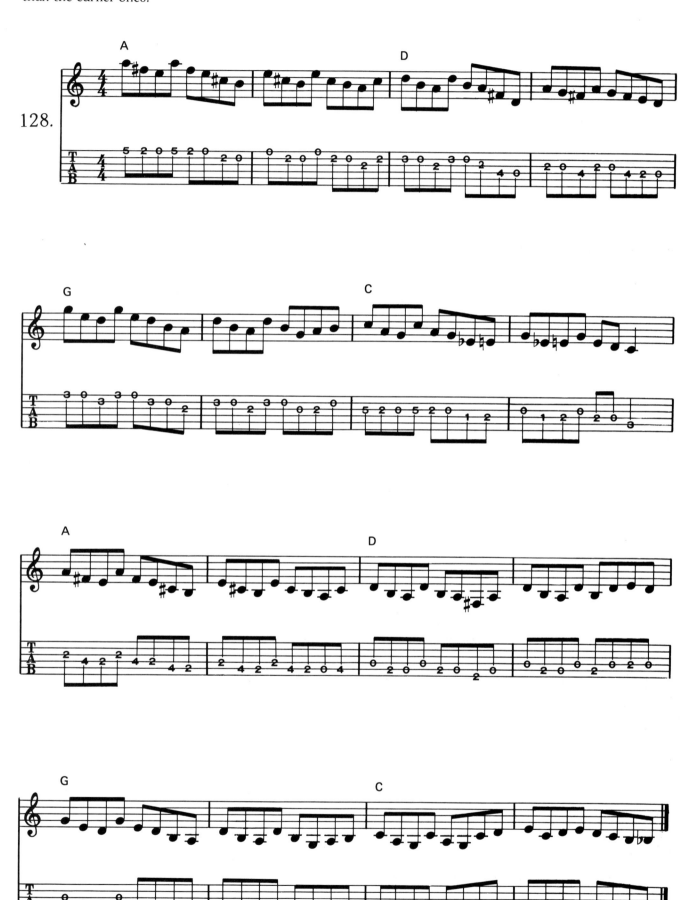

129.

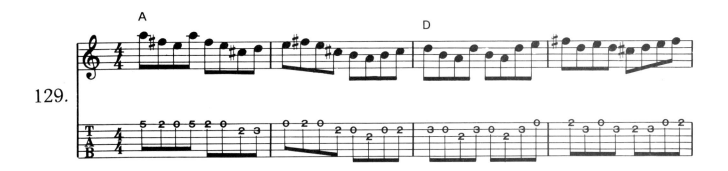

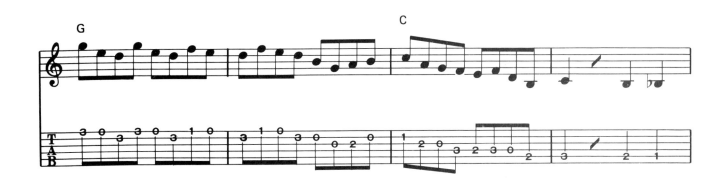

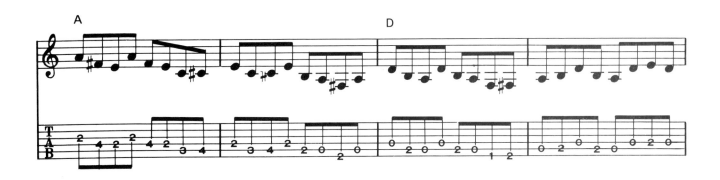

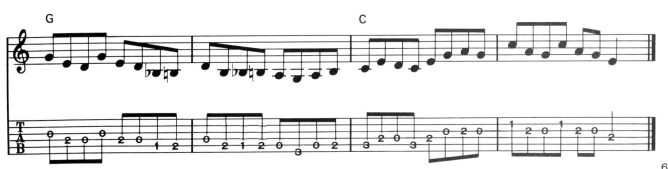

Of these two breaks from the second lick, the first one is straight, reproducing the seed lick with scrupulous accuracy. The second is freer; the seed lick functions as more of a starting point.

130.

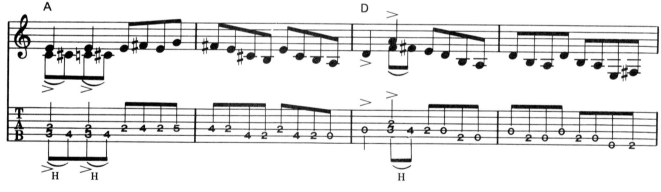

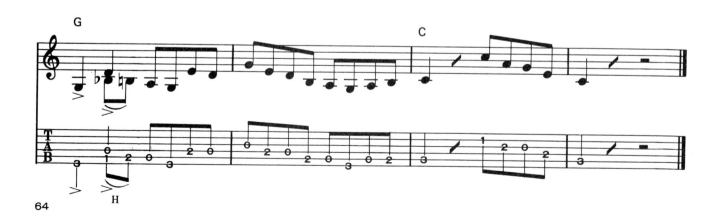

The third lick writ large explores the powerful technique of hitting two notes simultaneously and hammering on to one of them. This is a great way to emphasize a specific note and to add color to a solo.

See how many licks we generated from our original three? Although these breaks were intended simply to illustrate exploring, they show us some things about melodic sense as well.

Why does the second half of the break based on the first lick catch our ear more than the first half? Why, of the two breaks based on the second lick, is the second the more compelling? There is a progression in these breaks from the routine to the more interesting. In a way this progression mirrors the change in how a player works with licks over time, moving from strict imitations early on to freer and more flowing creations later. But the deeper point is that the passages that sound more interesting were fashioned with a solo-making perspective; that is, a view of the progression as a whole and consideration of the melody rather than just lick after lick.

Our melodic sense sometimes acts simply as a mediator, helping us to integrate whatever licks we find before us. Once developed it conditions our playing, always tugging us to not just play some licks but to fashion a solo.

# Jazz Kazoo

Another way to explore is to sing.

This is a super way because, as we mentioned earlier, our singing voices are blessed with a remarkable melodic sense. And you can literally tap this remarkable resource by consciously singing leads for songs you're working on and then trying to play the results. I call this the "jazz kazoo approach" because I tell people to let go and sing (or hum or whistle) as if they were playing solo in a jazz band.

Give yourself some time with this. Sometimes you'll sing something which sounds good when sung but which needs expanding if it is to work on the guitar. Work on it.

For example, I just sang

131.

and then augumented it into

132.

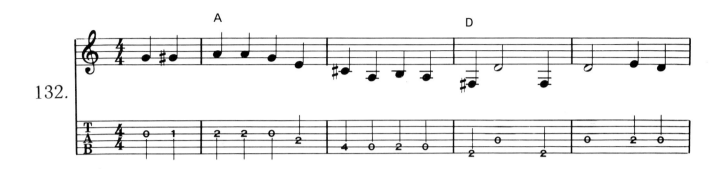

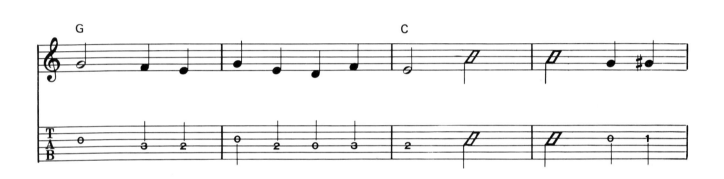

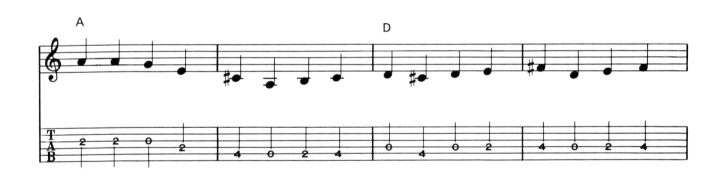

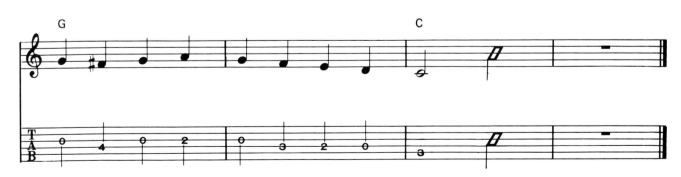

Given a little prodding, most people are inventive well beyond their own expectations. Not long ago I ordered one of my students, a scientifically-minded fellow whose guitar playing had been almost entirely imitative until then, to hum a jazz kazoo break for "Don't Let Your Deal Go Down" into my cassette recorder. The result:

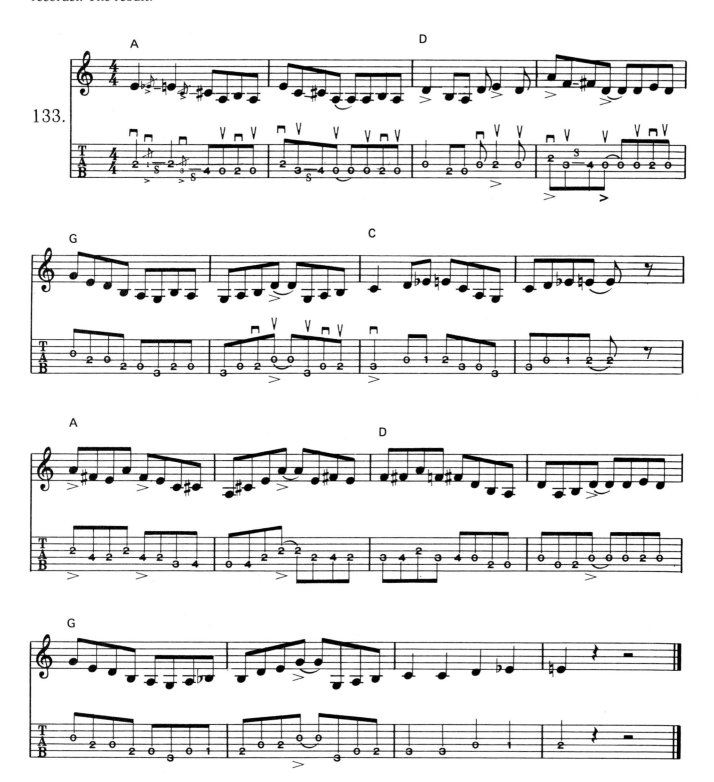

A finished solo! What we have here is neither the melody with some notes added nor an arcade of licks, but a beautiful complementary melody. A hybrid of the direct and the indirect.

Wonderful new licks and solos await the intrepid kazooist.

# Second Bonanza: Key of C

The phrases remain the same but the licks are different.

# Round Robin: C C F C, C C G G, and C C F F

134.

135.

136.

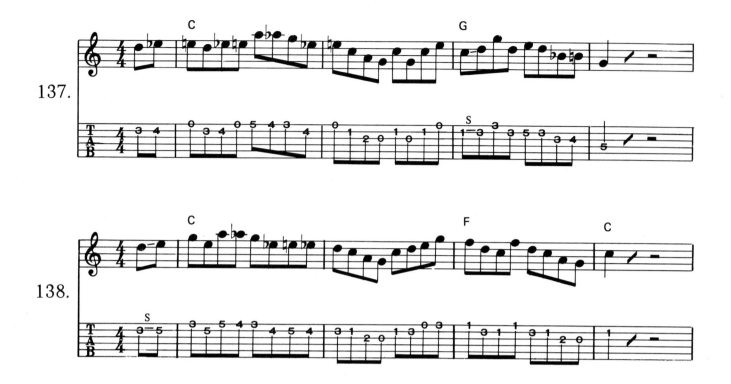

137.

138.

Crosspicking made interesting with a slide and a hammer in the G lick:

139.

The kind of jumps that are used often when playing up the neck appear in the C lick.

140.

If you haven't already noticed that the E♭ on the fourth fret of the B string is *the* popular weird note in the key of C then it's about time someone pointed it out to you.

141.

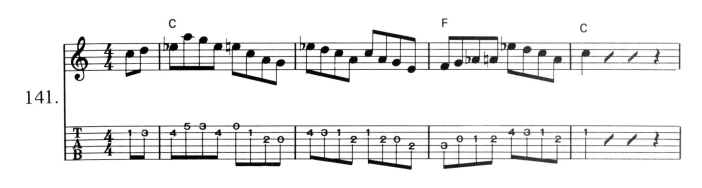

142.

143.

144.

145.

146.

A piquant F measure:

147.

Less is more sometimes, as we hear in the second half.

148.

149.

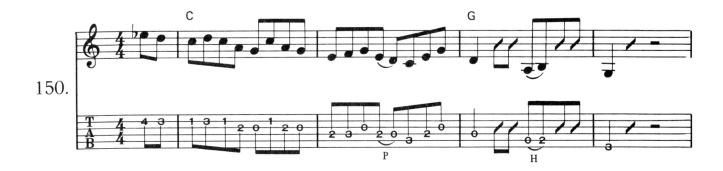

150.

Frisky:

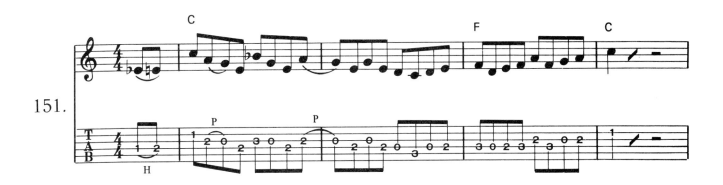

151.

If in our midst there is an alternative fingering for a note we often use, it usually pays to make its acquaintance—the C note on the G string for example.

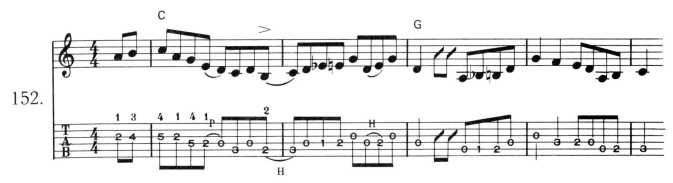

152.

On the banjo is where you've heard this F lick before.

The first seven notes are a classic anticipation to be commenced with a powerful upstroke.

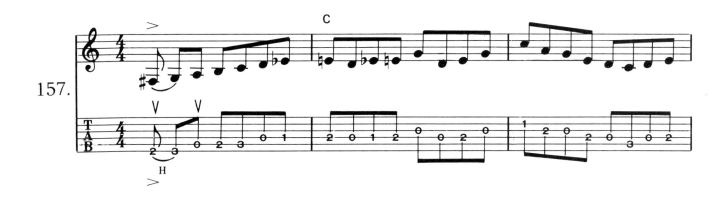

157.

Sounds like you've heard it before but you haven't.

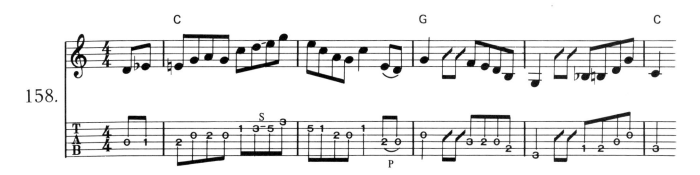

158.

Smart:

159.

160.

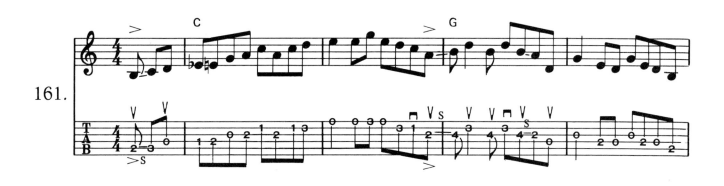

161.

162.

163.

**164.**

**165.**

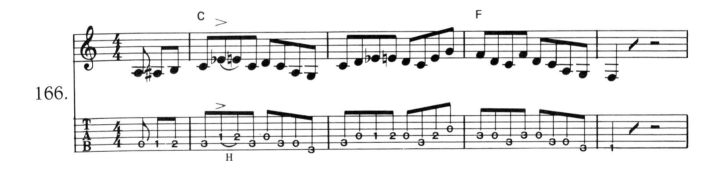

**166.**

Time to recalibrate again for one that starts at the top of the measure.

**167.**

**168.**

Two impeccable leads to wind up:

**169.**

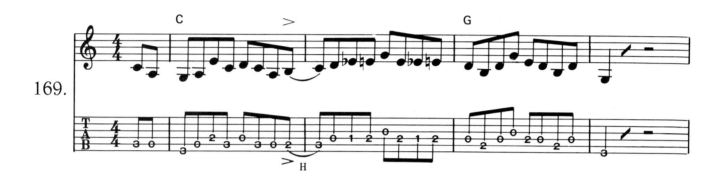

**170.**

Notice the symmetry of the pulloffs in this one.

# First Classic Ending Phrase:
# C G C C

175.

176.

177.

178.

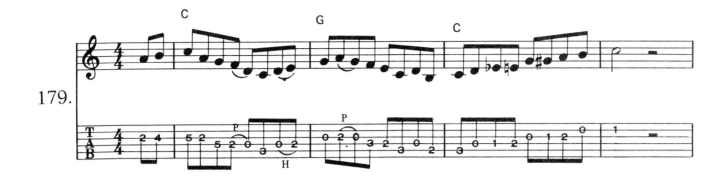

179.

The pinky gets a healthy workout at the beginning of this choice lead.

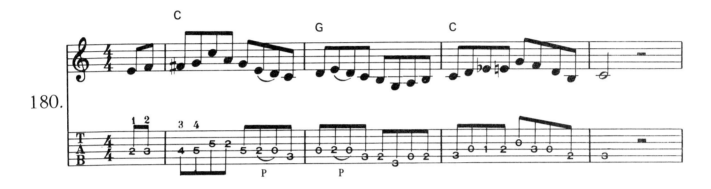

180.

A popular old-timey bass-run in the third measure:

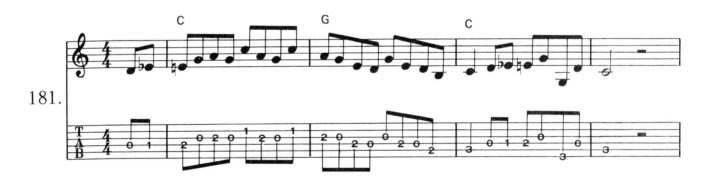

181.

182.

183.

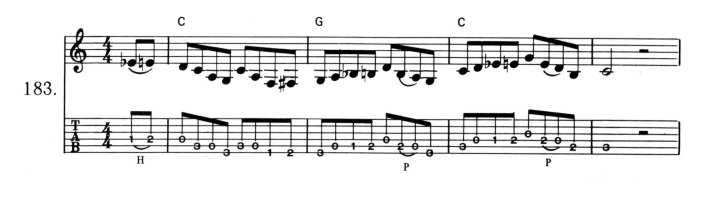

184.

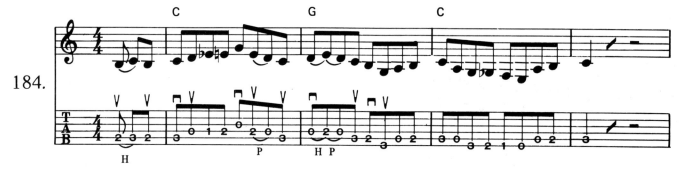

Playful:

185.

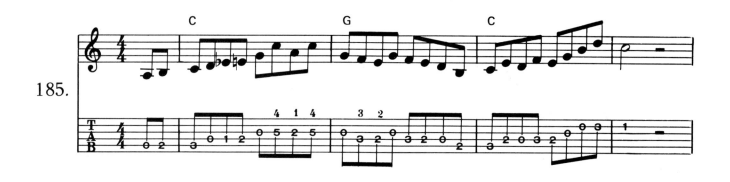

186.

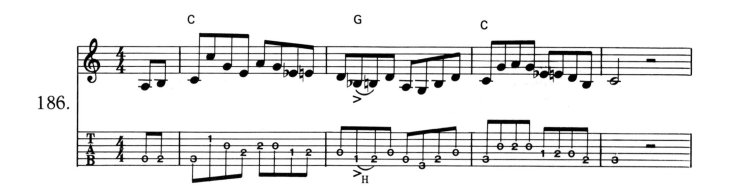

187.

A real sizzler:

188.

# Second Classic Ending Phrase: G G C C

189.

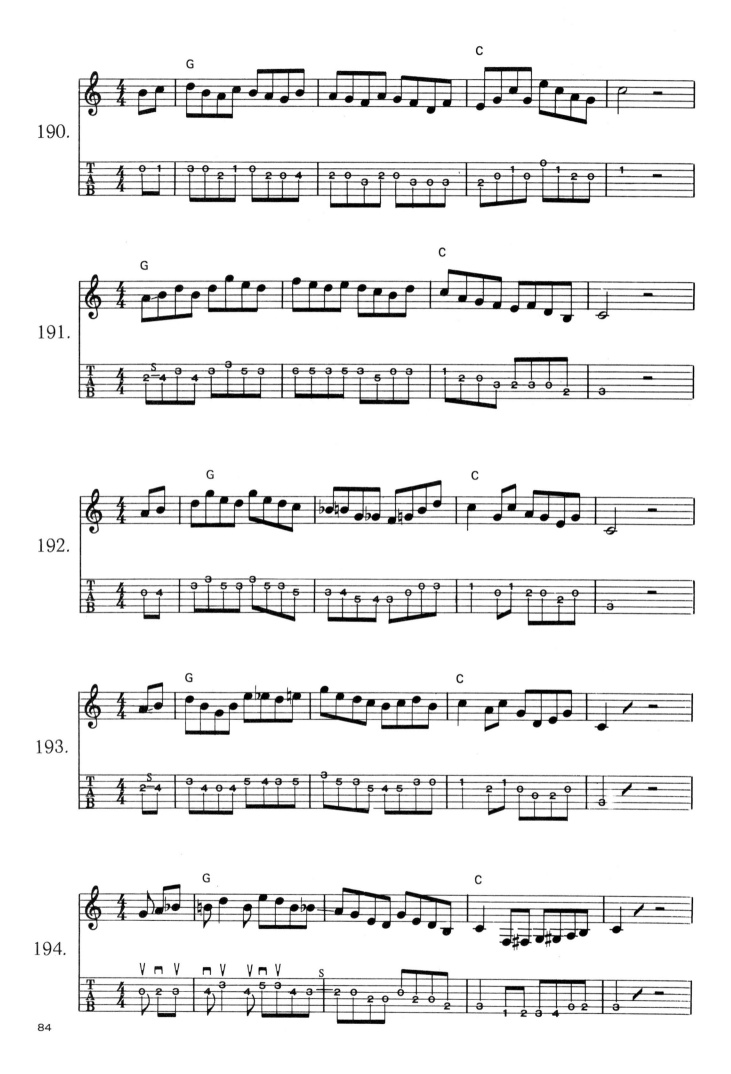

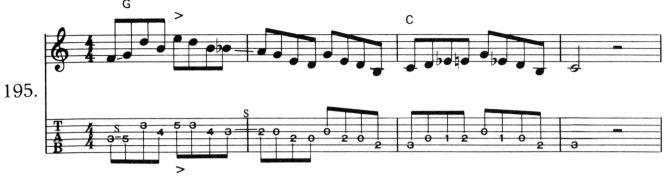

195.

Two that know how to have a good time:

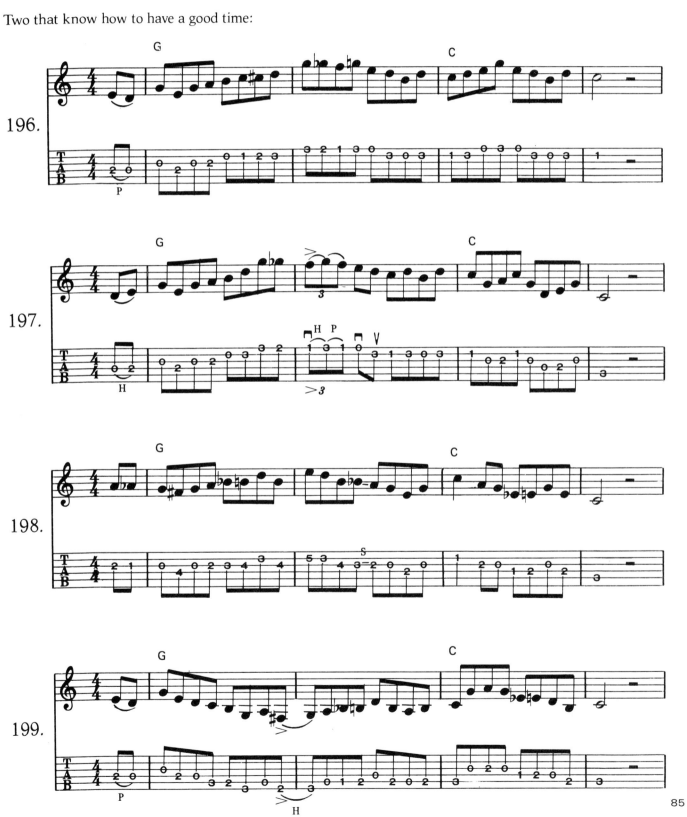

196.

197.

198.

199.

200.

201.

Lastly, a syncopated variation:

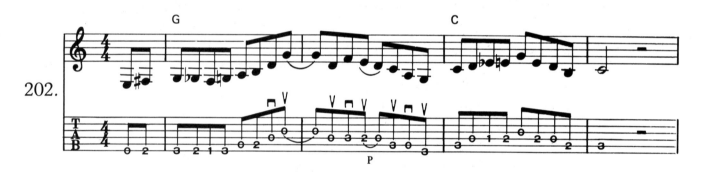

202.

**Tony Rice and Orrin Star**

# Bluesy Licks

Licks based on blues scales have a special power and are widely used in bluegrass. In fact, you would be hard pressed to find a bluegrass solo that did not include at least a couple flatted thirds or sevenths, and many of the licks we've already presented include them. But there are some great bluesy moves we haven't yet covered, and now's the time.

# Item One

Let's start with a Tony Rice lick. Tony is synonymous with hot bluesy playing, and this lick with him:

203.

This lick (first recorded as an ending) sounds best when played fast. You must also slow down on the last couple notes a little so that the strum with which it ends can be unhurried.

When I first heard this lick I remember having the same reaction as when I heard my first diminished run: Wow! Beaned by something out of left field. Today my reaction is more like "Oh yeah, those bluesy and minor notes from a G scale played in that certain pattern." You too will be on familiar terms with such sounds after you work through the licks in this chapter.

# "Little Maggie"

"Little Maggie" is a natural vehicle for bluesy licks since it has a bluesy melody.
Here is a solo for it that employs the sounds we just heard.

## Little Maggie

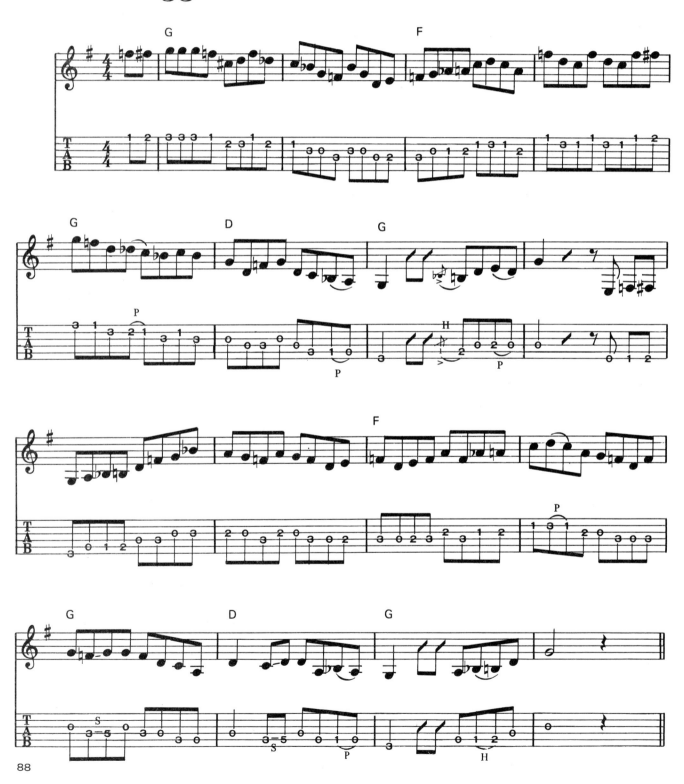

Moving from the specific to the more general, let's now look at bluesy licks for
the two underlying phrases in "Little Maggie."

## First Phrase: G G F F

This is a popular phrase which appears in many instrumentals as well as songs.

**208.**

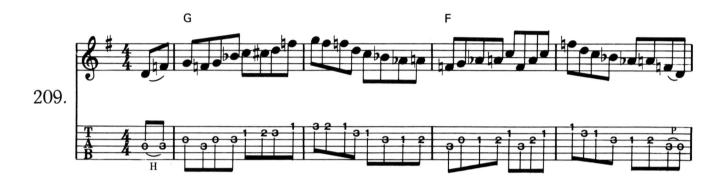

**209.**

Gary Mehalick uses this in "June Apple."

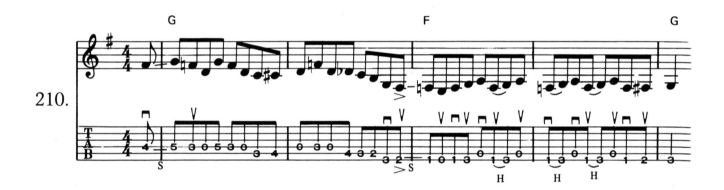

**210.**

First half courtesy of Anthony Rice:

**211.**

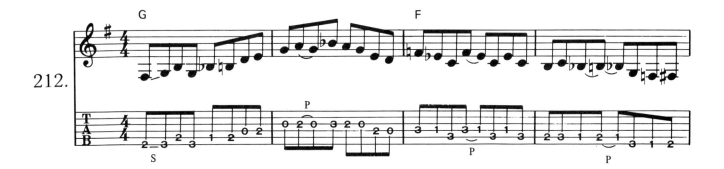

## Second Phrase: G D G G

Bluesy licks often have an interesting self-contained quality: They stay within
one basic scale and yet they work over changing chords. Like these first two:

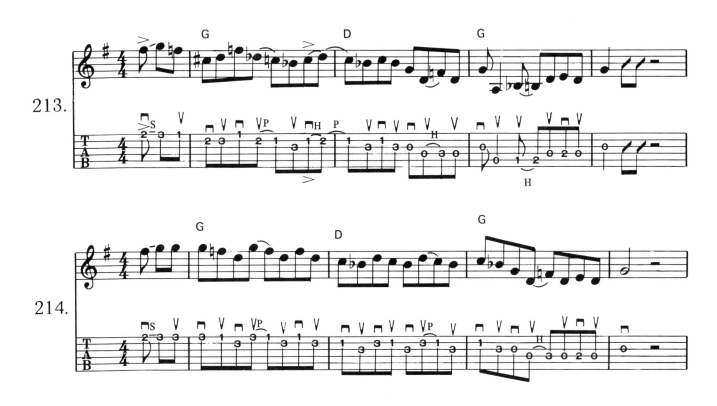

Doc played this in a "Little Maggie" solo.

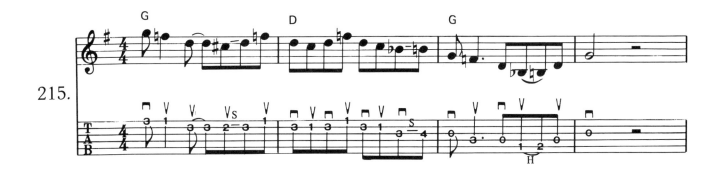

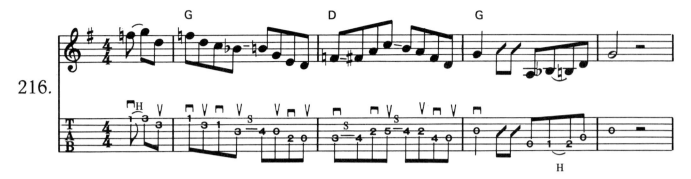

216.

In the style of Russ Barenberg, whose playing exhibits considerable blues power:

217.

218.

219.

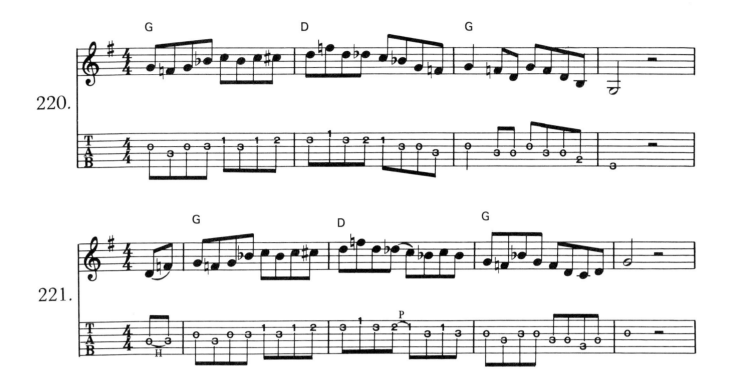

220.

221.

The G run at the end is a Clarence White trademark.

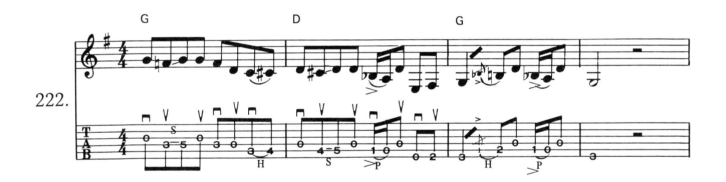

222.

As should be clear by now, hammers, pulls, and slides are the life of spice.

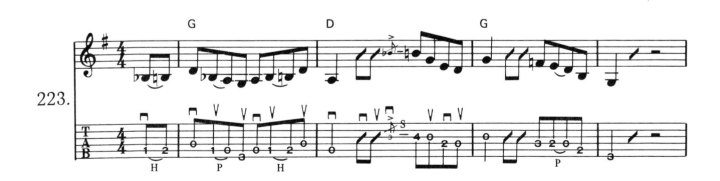

223.

# Clarence White's Special G Run

The late and great Clarence White developed a striking bluesy variation of the standard G-run, and it has become a flatpicking classic.

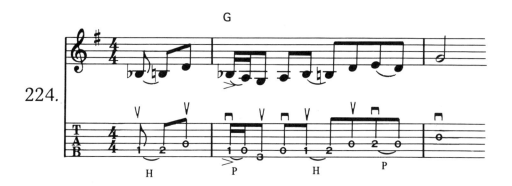

Clarence White in 1973

It is a versatile lick that can be used in a number of different ways.

Like the G-run it is based on, it is a punchy way to end a break.

225.

One reason this lick may already sound familiar to you is that Tony Rice, White's musical heir, ends almost all of his bluegrass solos with some form of it.

It is also a good opener, as we see in this G-to-D phrase from Mark O'Connor.

226.

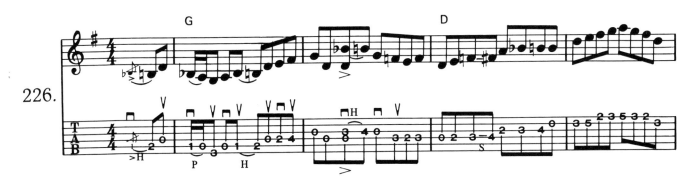

And the first half of the lick, which is its core, works almost anywhere. Here it is in two different locations in G measures.

227.

228.

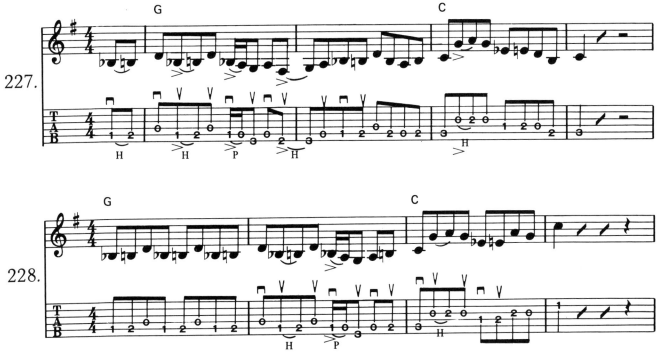

It works nicely in C as well.

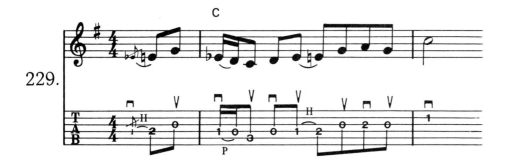

229.

It can also be used to anticipate the chord on which it is based. Here is the C version of the lick at the end of the *G* measure in a G-to-C phrase (also from Mark O'Connor).

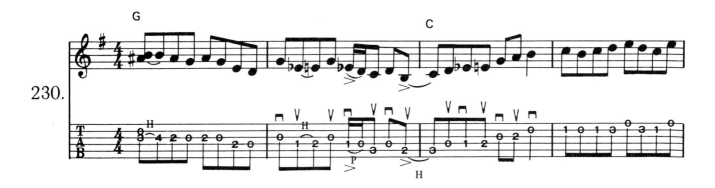

230.

# Trail-Offs

All bluegrass breaks end with some kind of tag—a lick that signals the end of a lead and that keeps things interesting while the melody is in repose.

For guitarists this usually means some kind of G run; having long ago surrendered to its charms, we often find it hard to imagine doing anything else at the end of a solo. But this is small-minded. As our brother fiddlers have shown, the tag zone can be a great playground, a special place to cut loose and romp. And it is the most fun when you stretch it out for an extra measure or two.

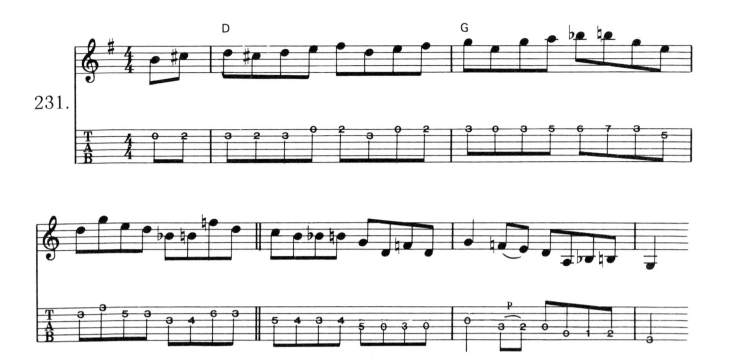

**231.**

I call these long-playing tags *trail-offs.* They belong in this chapter because they have a tradition of being bluesy. And what we have for you is a holiday assortment in the key of G. To play trail-offs with the proper feel, you need to keep in mind that they belong to ending phrases, and so we start each one with a short D lick.

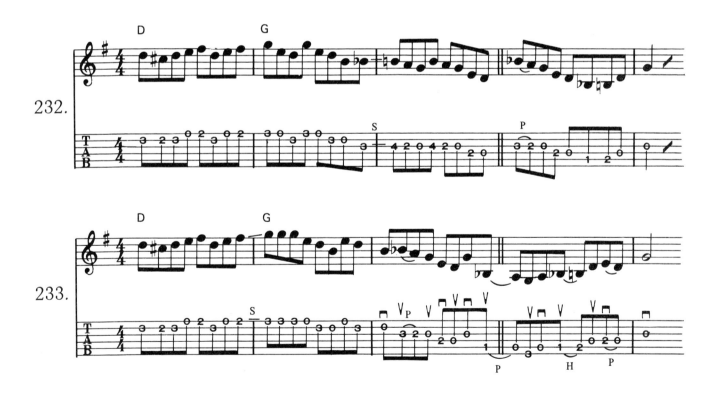

**232.**

**233.**

As you can see, trail-offs are not so much a new breed of lick as they are a new arena for combining familiar elements. Many of those that follow incorporate various beloved G runs and strums yet they sound fresh in this new setting.

My partner Gary provided this one. It also works in a G D G G ending phrase, which is how he actually uses it.

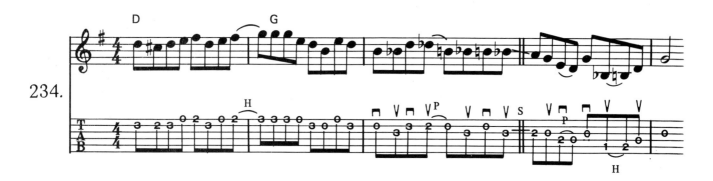

234.

Tony would approve:

235.

236.

237.

238.

239.

Clarence would approve:

240.

241.

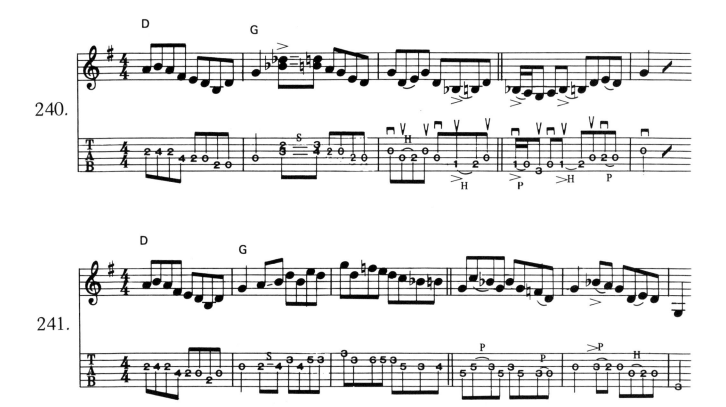

One of my very favorites:

242.

Two more now from master fiddler Bobby Hicks. This first one is an interesting
perpetual motion concept.

243.

The two breaks in the string of eighth notes contribute to the high finesse rating
of this next one.

244.

245.

# A Popular Mini-Phrase

Many fiddle tunes (like "Sally Goodin" and "Leather Britches") have a quick I V I chord change in their final measures. I noticed while I was researching licks for this book that bluesy licks were popular in these spots. In particular I noticed these two licks from Dan Crary,

246.

247.

these two from Tony Rice,

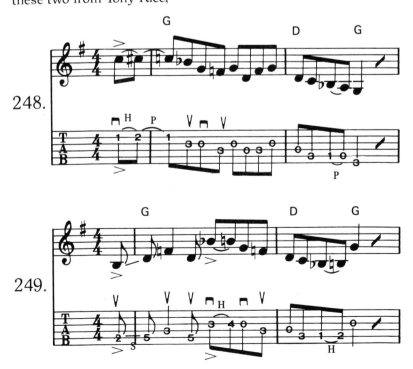

248.

249.

and this one from me.

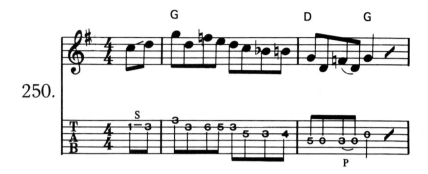

250.

# Item Last

Out now with another T. Rice infrared special—an ending that starts with a lick which, practically speaking, is the reverse of the Rice lick with which we opened this chapter (and one which has graced many a "Freeborn Man" introduction). I helped assemble the last two measures, but the sound is pretty much pure Tony.

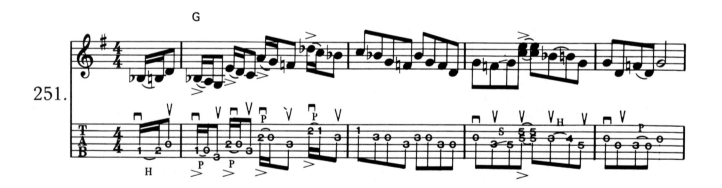

251.

# Closed Licks: Up the Neck and Other Delights

*Closed licks* are licks which use no open strings. Their beauty is their flexibility: Each closed lick may be played in different keys simply by placing it higher or lower on the neck. The secret is the handful of closed positions on which these licks are based.

*Closed positions* are orderly grids of notes with specific fingerings that are ours to launch licks from once we become familiar with them. The good news is that these positions behave like the basic chord-fingerings we already know and respect; the challenging news is that you need to put your pinky on active duty and to know more about the fingerboard at large in order to use them. But we're here to help.

# The Positions

Grids of notes with fingerings are easier to play from than to talk about because there is no established way of describing the various positions, at least not in bluegrass circles. ("Oh yeah, that one," while popular, does not quite qualify.) After considerable meditation and nail loss, we have assembled our own varied approach which we'll explain now as we proceed with the first of five positions we will identify.

### The E-Bar

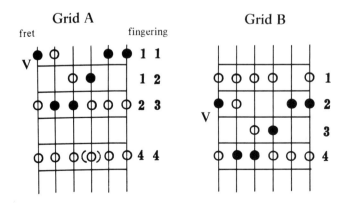

This position contains two basic grids and we have outlined them both in the diagrams above using the notes of the major scale. Here is how they look in linear fashion if we plant ourselves on the fifth fret.

**Grid A:**

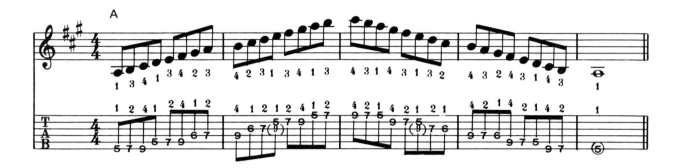

**Grid B:**

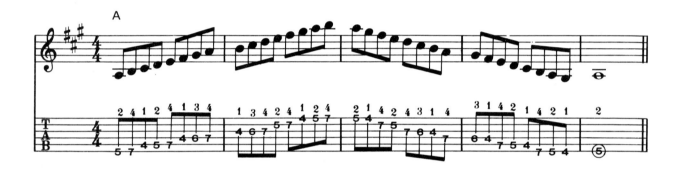

On first viewing, these scales might appear to be alien collections of notes but in fact they are organized in ways that are not unfamiliar to you. All that's needed is a little recognition. Enter the implied chord:

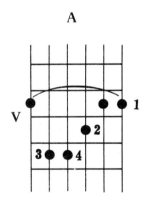

Each closed position implies a chord which is in effect a barred version of an open chord. This familiar shape can be a vital reference helping you to see the order within a position and to recognize that it is the same order as one you've been using since you started with the guitar.

To encourage this awareness we have named each position according to this chord. This is the *E-bar* position since its chord has the form of an E on top of the index finger's *bar.*

Playing fiddle tunes in closed position is a great way to scope out the scales and fingerings that outline a position. Below, for example, is the latter half of a "Billy in the Lowground" A-part played in each of the three fingerings under the jurisdiction of the E-bar. We have planted it on the eighth fret to yield the key of C, where the tune is traditionally played. Take your time and follow the fingering designations carefully keeping in mind that this is an exercise and not necessarily a practical way to play this tune.

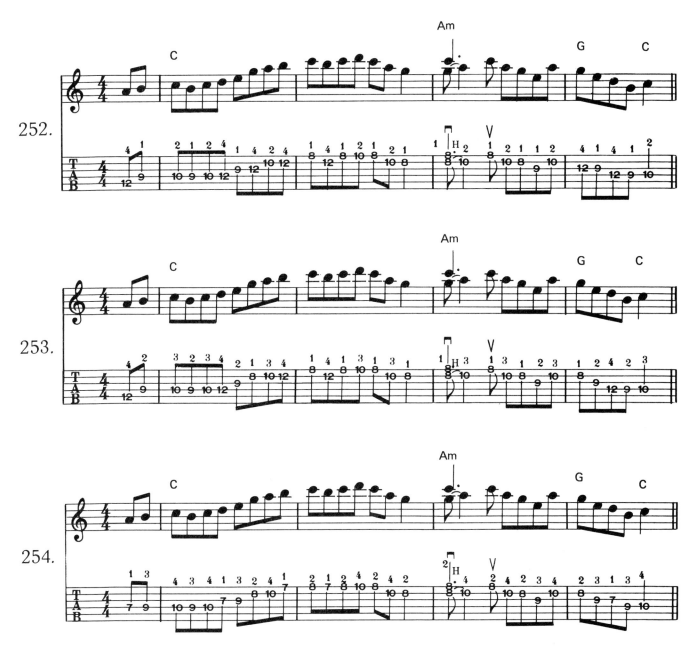

In practice, our sense of a closed position revolves around the portion of the position that feels good to hold and play from. We often discover and use this area long before we understand the full position, and the *mini-bar* we find ourselves making becomes our working symbol of the position.

**Grid A Mini-bar**

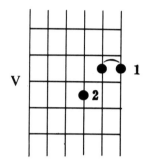

The mini-bar within Grid A is one we already know since we invoke it in many of the G licks we play and since it is fingered like an F chord. Placing it on the fifth fret, here are a couple doodles around it.

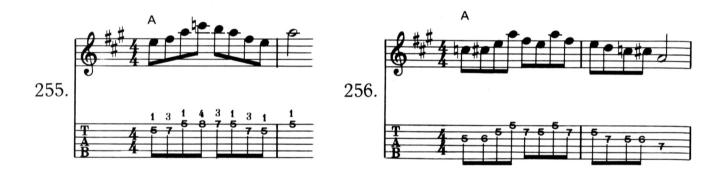

255.                                           256.

Grid B has no corresponding mini-bar as such but I find myself thinking in terms of this three-fingered construction.

**Grid B Mini-bar**

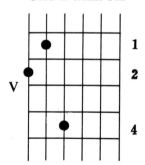

Here are some fifth-fret doodles for it just the same.

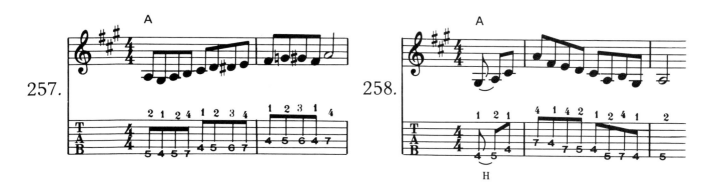

Now that we have the outlines, let's have a look around the position. Ending-type riffs—those that hang on a single chord for the better part of two measures—seem to be ideal for this.

This first one shows just how much you can accomplish with three fingers on three consecutive frets (which is what makes the E-bar such a popular position).

Here is more of the same with a little lesson in pragmatic fingering.

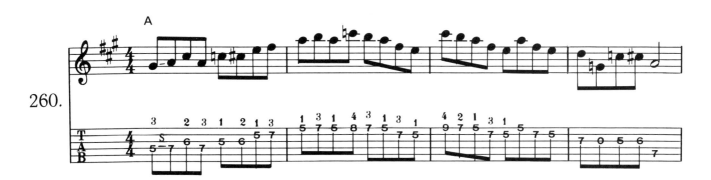

A couple riffs on Grid B now:

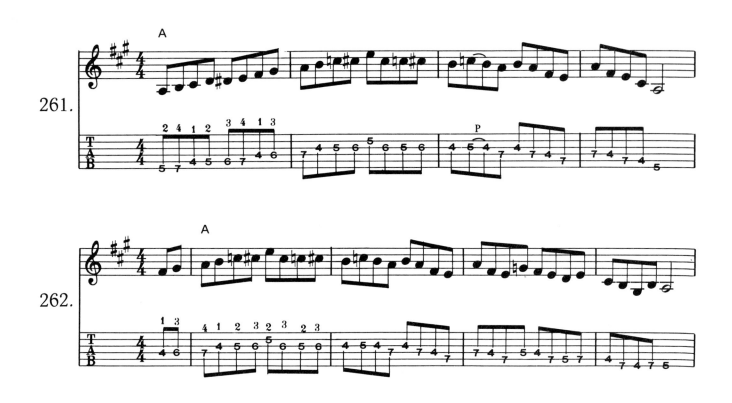

261.

262.

Often it feels best to shift between grids.

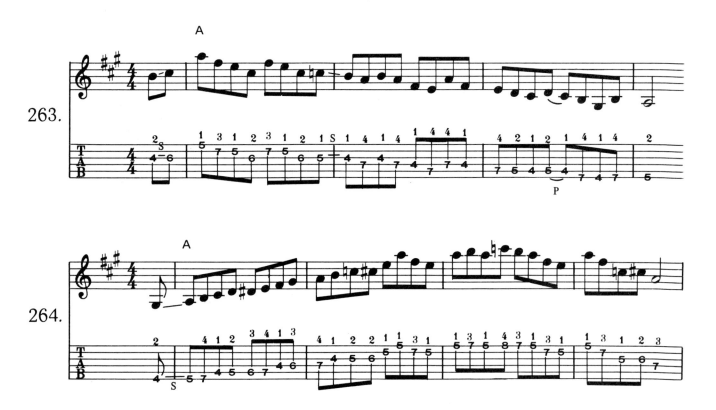

263.

264.

Shifts like these occur all the time in closed-position playing because no single grid can offer the most manageable fingerings available for any given tune.

## The A-Bar

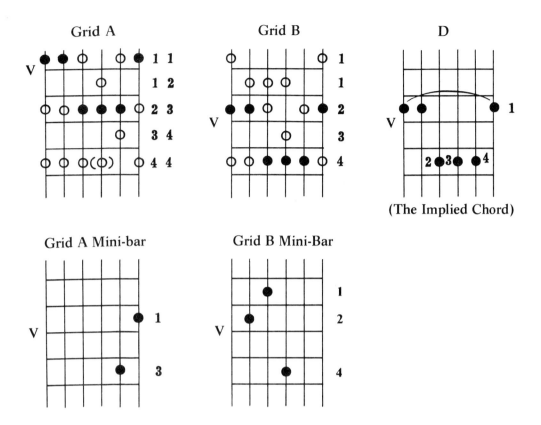

Grid A          Grid B          D

Grid A Mini-bar     Grid B Mini-Bar

(The Implied Chord)

Similarly contoured and also implying two different basic grids, the A-bar is the sister position to the E-bar.

The basic scales with the bar on fret five*:

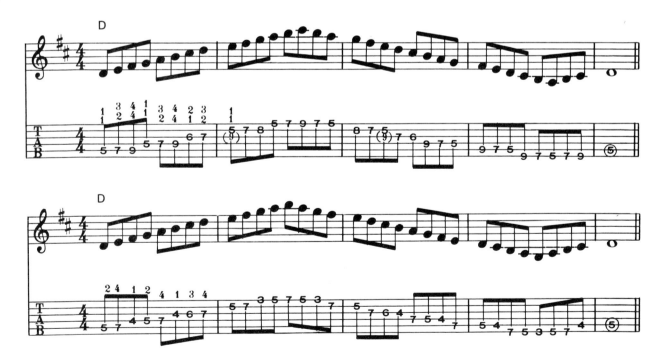

*We plant positions on the fifth fret in many of the examples in this chapter simply because it is a convenient location in the middle of the fingerboard.

Excerpt from "Billy in the Lowground" with bar on fret three (for key of C):

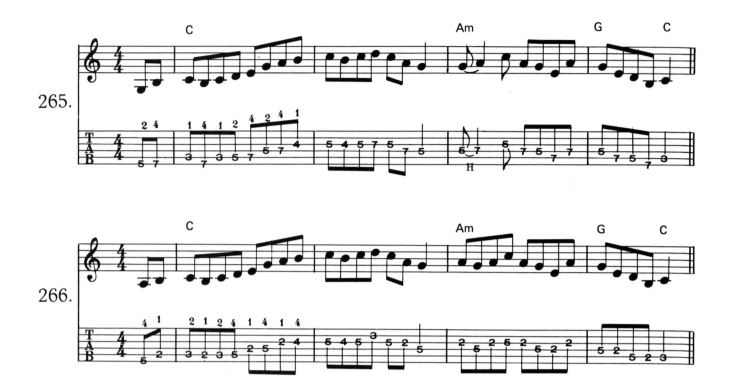

265.

266.

Note the pragmatic imperative at work: (a) We did not present the other fingering option for Grid A because this tune works out to be so pinky intensive in this position that it would not be feasible to use, and (b) we could not accomplish the hammeron given the parameters of Grid B so we devised a suitable variation. Fingerings themselves often lead us to appealing new sounds.

Grid-A mini-bar doodles:

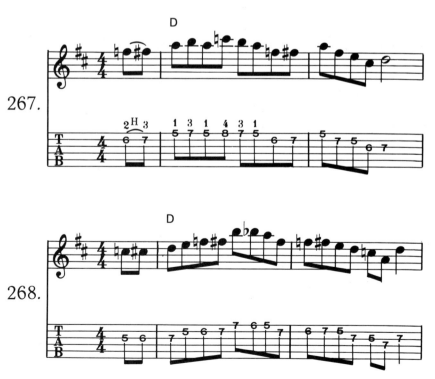

267.

268.

Grid-B mini-bar doodles:

269.

270.

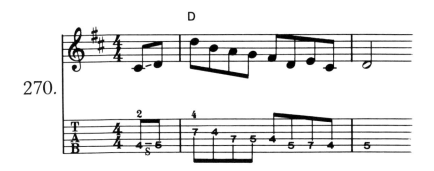

Longer, ending-like doodles:

271.

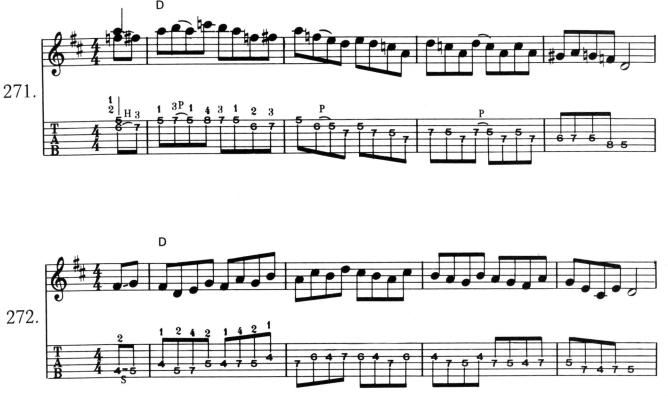

272.

And a bipartisan one:

273.

## The G-Bar

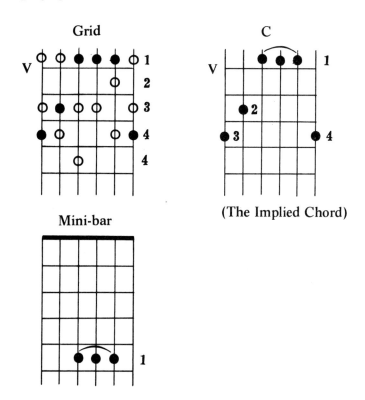

Grid

C

(The Implied Chord)

Mini-bar

Because so much of our playing occurs around open G and C chords, the barred versions of these chords have a special importance: They are the keys to translating many of our favorite open licks into closed licks, and they stand out as the positions that can best help us to see the connection that exists between a closed position and its open counterpart.

Basic scale with bar on fifth fret:

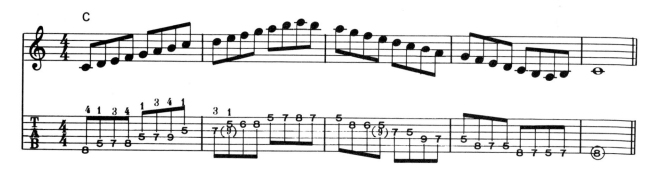

C

"Billy in the Lowground" excerpt (also on fifth fret, for the key of C):

274.

The mini-bar here is simply the index finger across the first four strings. Like most mini-bars, it does not appear in actual use every time those strings are played but only when certain fingerings (usually moves between the D and G strings) are needed. Doodles:

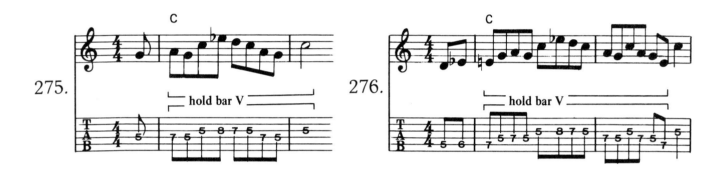

275.

276.

Ending doodles:

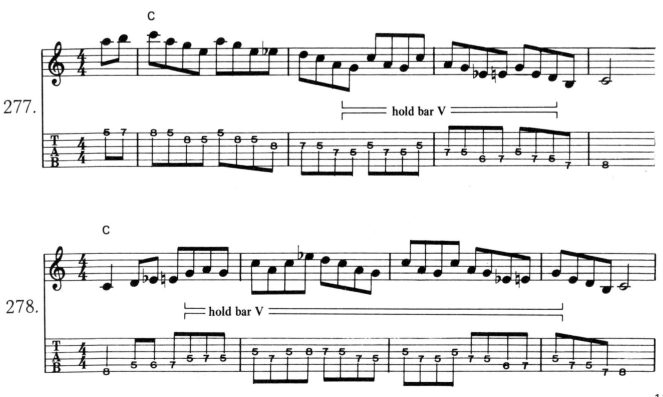

277.

278.

It's fun to slide into a position from a note out of the position.

279.

As you can see, playing over a G-bar is exactly like playing over an open G chord except that the fingers are shifted down a fret. The story is the same with all closed positions.

## The C-Bar

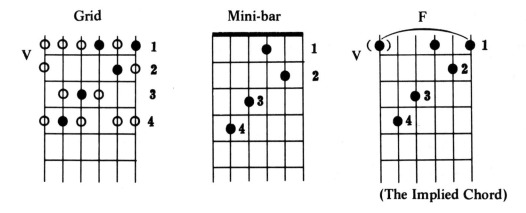

Grid | Mini-bar | F

(The Implied Chord)

The C-bar is one of the most satisfying closed positions because it spans only four frets and because its mini-bar is practically a complete replica of the open chord, making the open-closed connection obvious.

The scale at the fifth fret:

"Billy in the Lowground" at the twelfth fret (key of C, one octave above the open chord):

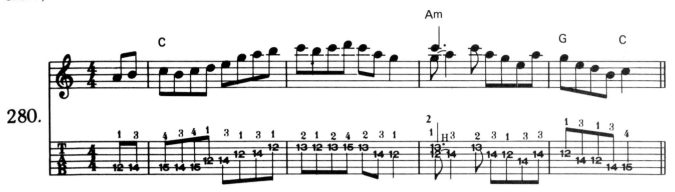

**280.**

Since the mini-bar is practically the full closed chord, we need not doodle diminutively. Here are the ending riffs.

**281.**

**282.**

If this position feels somehow familiar, that's because it is, at least in part: Most of the D licks we play are based on a C-bar at the second fret as well as on the open D.

# The D-Bar

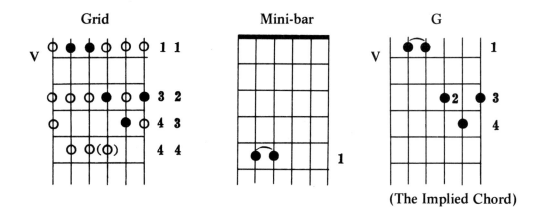

Grid          Mini-bar          G

V                                V

(The Implied Chord)

With its pinky-heavy architecture and no real mini-bar to speak of on the treble end, the D-bar is probably the least convenient closed position to use by itself. But parts of it are very good to work with, particularly when used in tandem with parts of the E-bar below or the C-bar above, and so it is not to be overlooked.

Fifth-fret scale:

"Billy in Lowground" (tenth fret for C):

283.

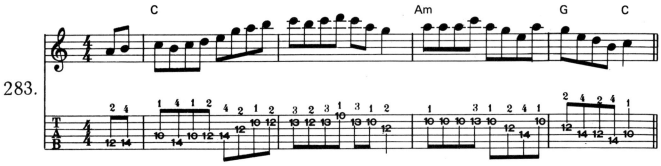

The bona-fide mini-bar is on the low end of the position. It is the same index-finger mini-bar that appears in the G-bar except one string over, as in:

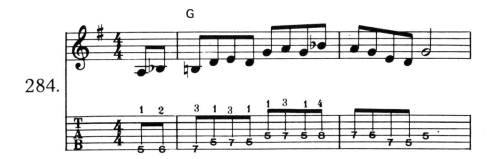

Over on the treble end we have some handy patterns built around the triangle that is the heart of the D chord.

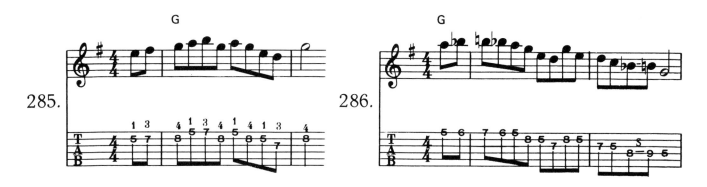

We shift into the other fingering now for this funky blues pattern.

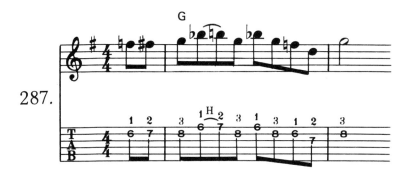

Turning now to our endings, one handy way to stay within this position and to be able to do some moving around is to shift between its two fingerings, as in this bluesy line.

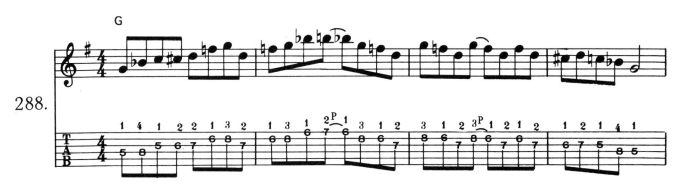

But, manageable fingerings being the priority that they are, shifting to a lower or higher position is often the most natural thing to do.

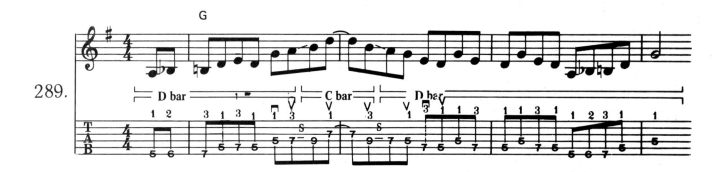

This shifting between positions is no different from the shifting we did between the two grids within the E-bar and the A-bar. As we mentioned earlier—and as we'll explore in a moment—such shifts are the norm in actual closed position playing.

# The Network

Now that we've defined our five positions, the next step is to look at how they lie in various keys and in relation to each other.

As you know from playing licks like these, three frets to the north of a G position lies an E position. This relationship is part of the very order of the guitar itself, and holds true anywhere on the neck. In fact, each position has an equally fixed relationship to these two and to each other; they are linked in a network.

You got a taste of how the network lines up vertically from the sequence of position placements that we used in order to play our five "Billy in the Lowground" excerpts in the key of C. All together, and in order, they appear as follows: Open C chord, A-bar at the third fret, G-bar at the fifth, E-bar at the eighth, D-bar at the tenth, and C-bar at the twelfth.

As a start to understanding what this means, try actually playing all of these chord positions in this order. And here is a pair of licks which together straddle the network. We identify the component positions within each lick like so: EV means E-bar at the fifth fret.

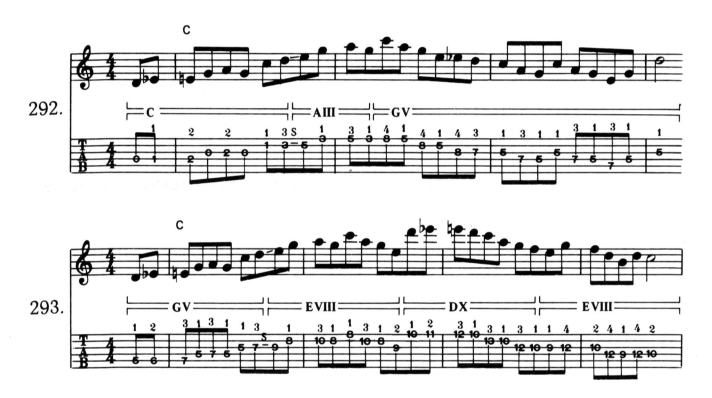

For a different chord the network shifts accordingly but the order within remains the same. Here, for example, is how it looks around a G: Open G chord, E-bar at the third fret, D-bar at the fifth, C-bar at the seventh, A-bar at the tenth, and G-bar at the twelfth.

Same network, new location. Here are the same multi-position licks in their new locations.

**295.**

Horizontally, closed positions relate like chords at the bottom of the neck: Just as G chords relate to C chords and A chords relate to D chords, so G-bars relate to C-bars and A-bars relate to D-bars on the same fret. For example, if you take a passage like

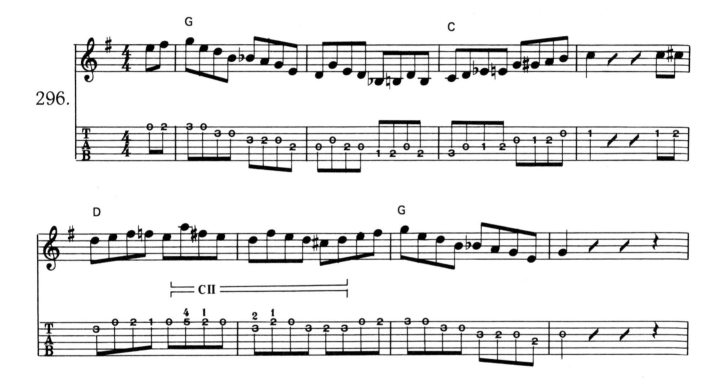

**296.**

and shift it up a couple frets

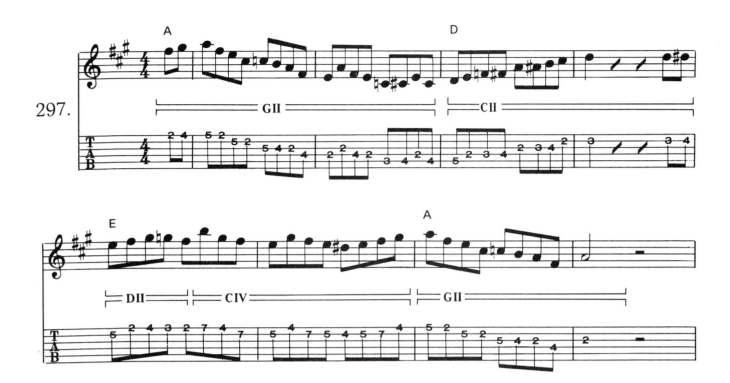

297.

the key changes (to A) but the horizontal relationships do not.

Yet one's horizontal neighbors don't exist in isolation; they too are part of a parallel vertical chain. You need to be aware of the whole thicket of relationships in a given region before you can really move around.

Beanblossom, 1971

# All Together Now

Here are ten leads for a I IV V I progression (with an extended V and an abbreviated final I) which highlight the range of motion that true closed-position play invites. Each lead is launched from a closed position on the fifth fret, and this starting position is varied every third lead so that all five of the closed positions appear there.

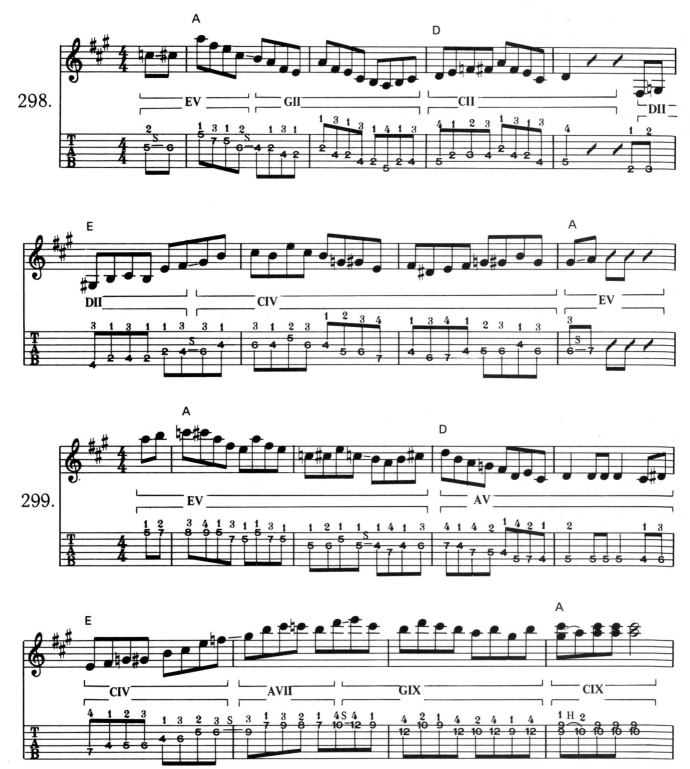

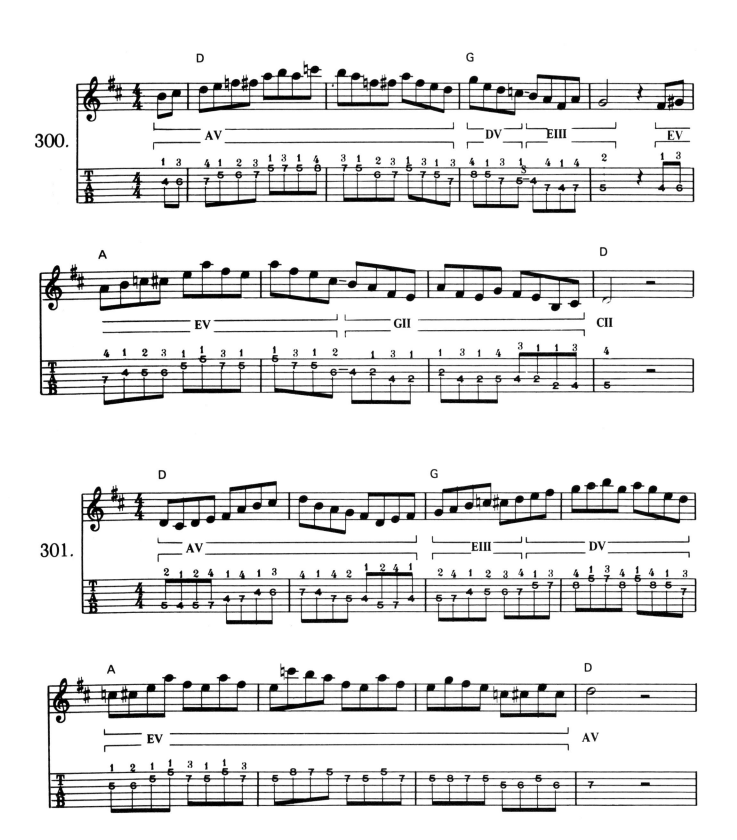

Deciding how to shift between fingerings, and between positions at large, is one of the chief creative challenges of playing closed since it is possible to move up or down at almost every point in a position. Some of my favorite moves appear in these examples; you'll discover yours as you play.

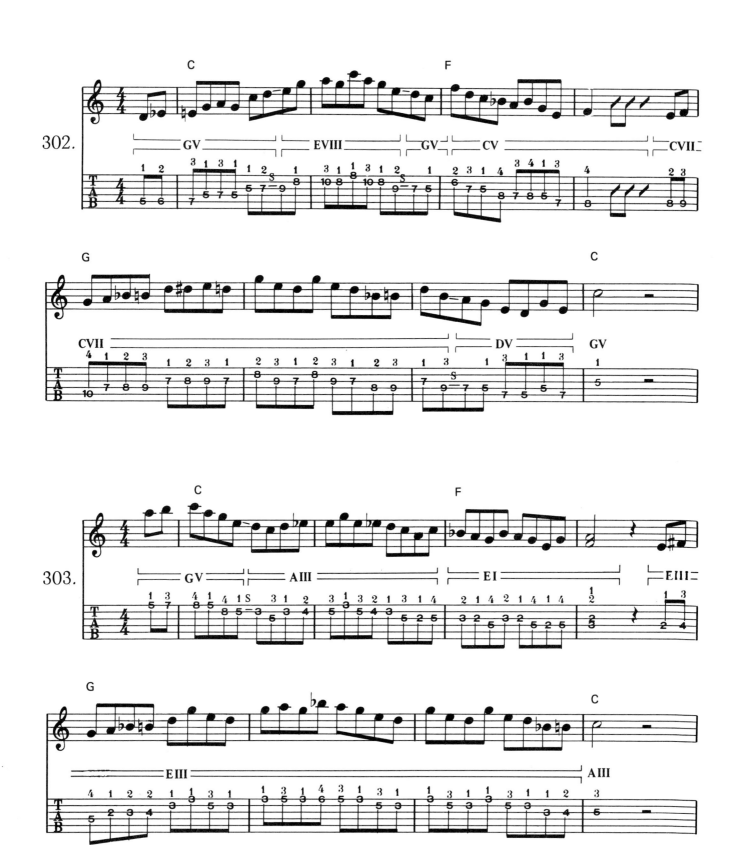

302.

303.

304.

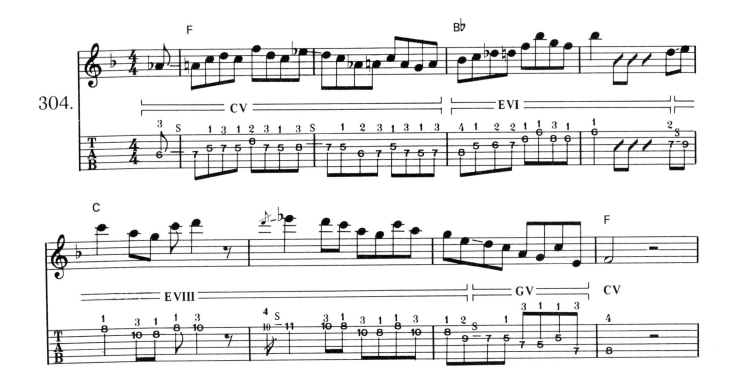

305.

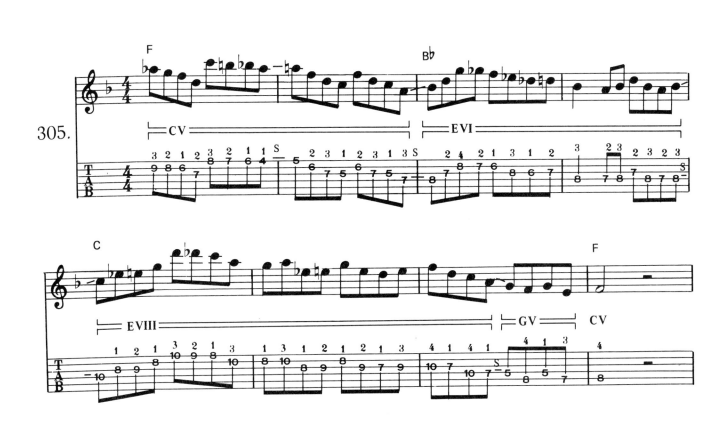

As you can see, the reality of closed-position playing is not one of loyalty to individual positions and of digital heroics, but one of preferred fingerings and position shifts. For the simple fact is that all players—even those skilled at pinky deployment—lean toward sounds that are comfortable to play.

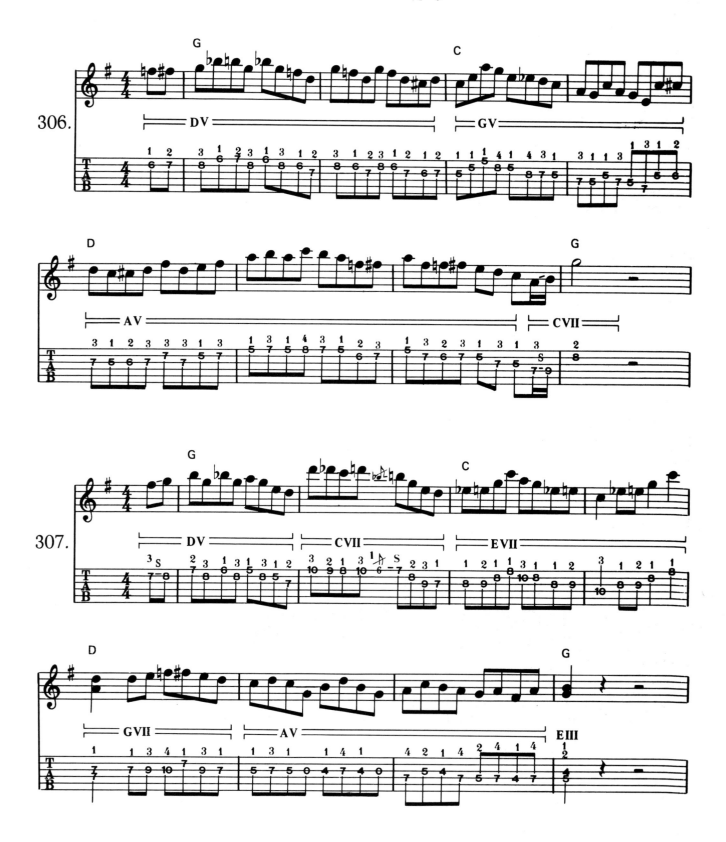

Once you move up the neck, a world of new and wider options appears before you. We've sketched out this world as best we can but this is just a start. A true sense of its dimensions and of your preferences within it is only achieved over time, in the course of playing.

Give yourself this time. Study the examples carefully. And if you feel discouraged at some point, remember: This business of playing from closed positions is something which mandolin players do as a matter of course (which is how they manage to do without capos)—and if they can do it, so can you.

Tut Taylor and David Bromberg in 1972

# Special Effects

We'll round out our bluegrass guitar menu now with a look at some of the special moves that flatpickers use to warm up their solos. Though some of these moves have appeared in some of the preceding licks, we've not yet considered them on their own terms or in depth.

# Crosspicking

*Crosspicking* refers to the syncopated rolls flatpickers use to imitate a fiddler's shuffle. It is a colorful technique that can lend drama to a solo and which has a wide range of potential uses.

The most popular crosspicking pattern consists of a two-measure set of forward rolls on three strings combined with some modest left-hand movements. The "Beaumont Rag" shuffle is one of the classic examples:

Tony Rice and Doc Watson at the Great American Music Hall in
San Francisco, April 1983

# Beaumont Rag

There is more than one way to pick such patterns. I recommend strict down/up alternation because I have found it to be the most comfortable method but others favor other approaches; such as, down-up-down/down-up-down; or, down-down-up/down-down-up. Though you will find that you settle on one main approach, it pays to familiarize yourself with other options as well since they each offer a slightly different sound.

To give you an idea of how much ground you can cover with the basic shuffle, let's turn to one of my favorite havens of pure crosspicking, the A-part of "June Apple." Here are four different interpretations.

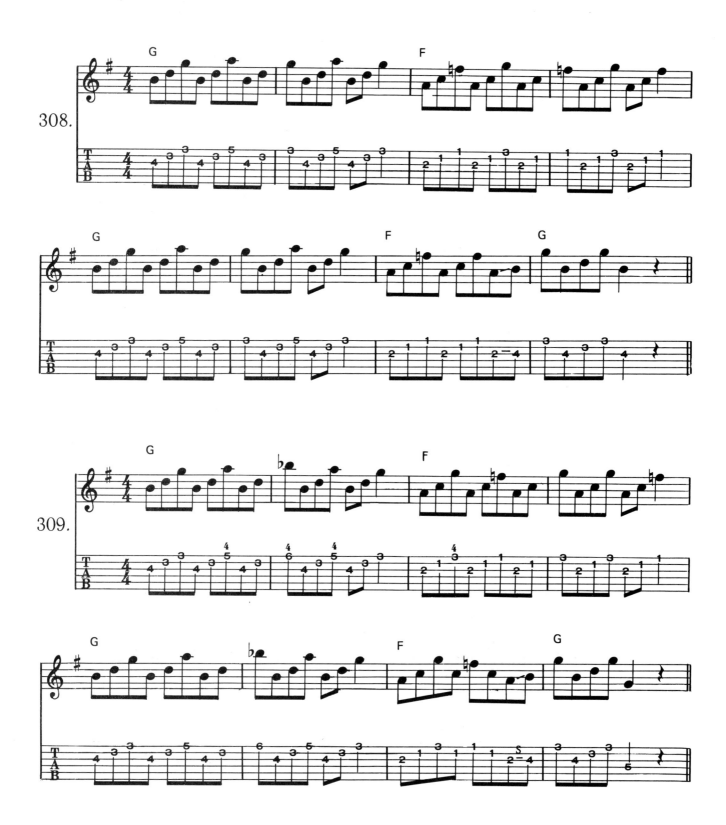

**310.**

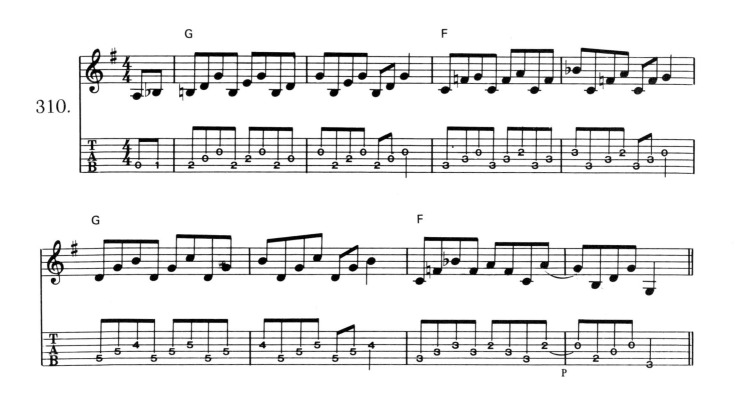

**311.**

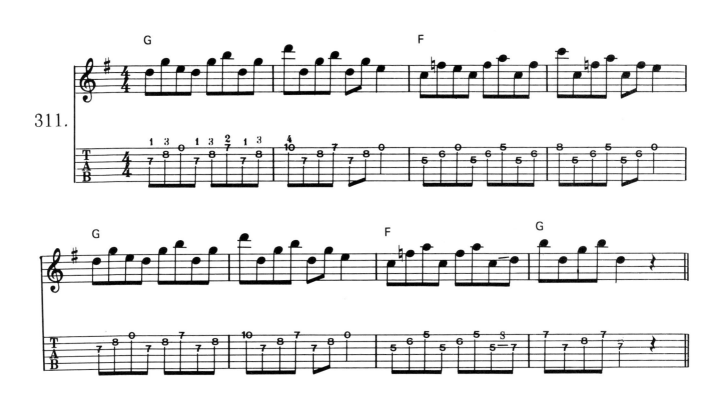

By varying the basic shuffle, further sets of options can be summoned. Here are three distinct variations.

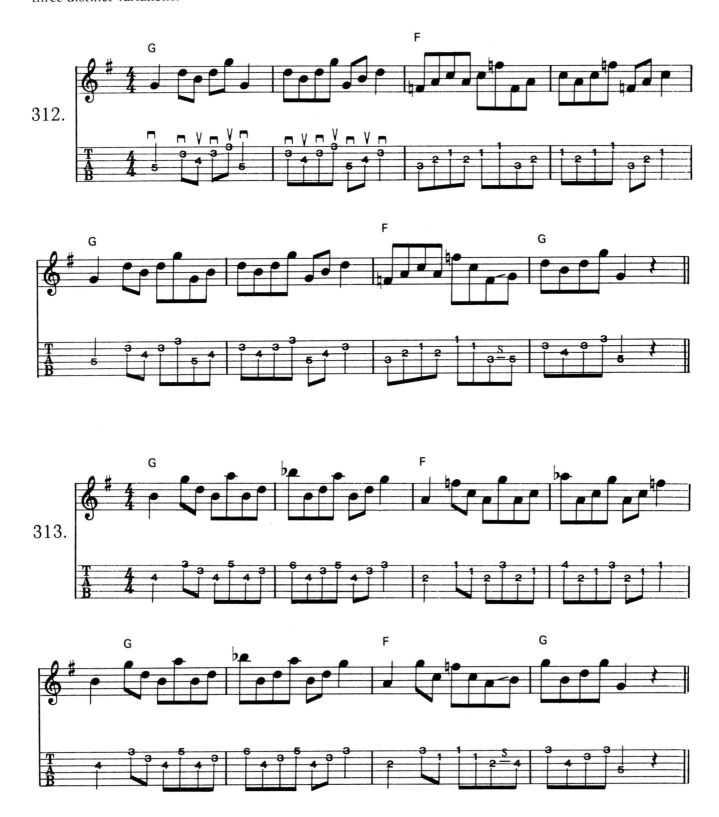

This down-up-up picking motion was pioneered on the mandolin by Jesse McReynolds but is a natural for the guitar as well.

314.

Speaking of variety, have you noticed the final two measures in each of these examples? Because of the chord change in the middle, the picking there departs from the established routine, introducing slides and other modifications in order to resolve gracefully. Such departures are essential because it is only by altering and adapting patterns to suit the needs of specific songs that you can meet the true challenge of crosspicking: how to get the most melodic mileage from an appealing yet essentially mechanical technique.

Here's a high mileage solo for "Don't Let Your Deal Go Down" in the key of G.

# *Don't Let Your Deal Go Down*

369.

As you may detect from this solo, part of the crosspicking challenge is deciding just *how much* to crosspick in a given break. For crosspicking works not only by itself but in various combinations with regular linear playing as well. And with the exception of those few songs that have it built into their melodies, crosspicking has no predetermined role in any song; it is up to you to decide the extent of its presence. Once you develop a feel for crosspicking, such decisions flow naturally. But the issue is never cut-and-dried. Consider the A-part of "June Apple" once more.

As you know from most of the preceding examples, I like to crosspick it entirely. But this is simply one among several options; another player (or even the same player in a different moment of inspiration) could just as easily hear the ideal crosspicking formula in something like

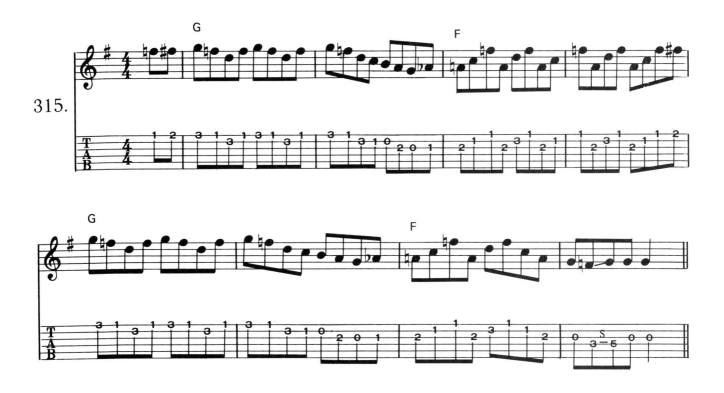

315.

Crosspicking also works in smaller doses—as an embellishment in the first measure of "Cherokee Shuffle" for example.

*Before:*

316.

135

*After:*

317.

In standard everyday bluegrass phrases I find that crosspicking lends itself to the V chord. For example, the I V phrase:

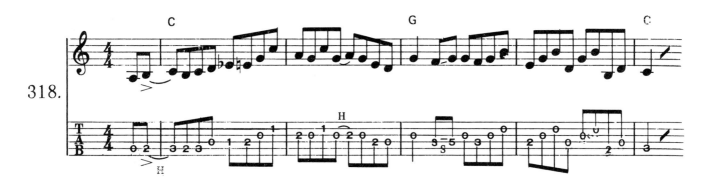

318.

Or the V I ending phrase:

319.

320.

As you can see from these examples, the more you adapt crosspicking to serve a melodic purpose (in these cases, simply the sound of the phrase), the less mechanical it tends to become. Such flexible usage has broadened the concept of crosspicking so that it includes picking in which motion between strings is maintained yet which does not adhere to one set pattern. Much of Norman Blake's playing is like this.

Bringing us full circle, here's a second, more kinetic "Beaumont Rag" solo (part of the version I played at Winfield in '76) that goes the distance with the basic shuffle and then resolves with some freer-form Blake-like picking.

# Beaumont Rag

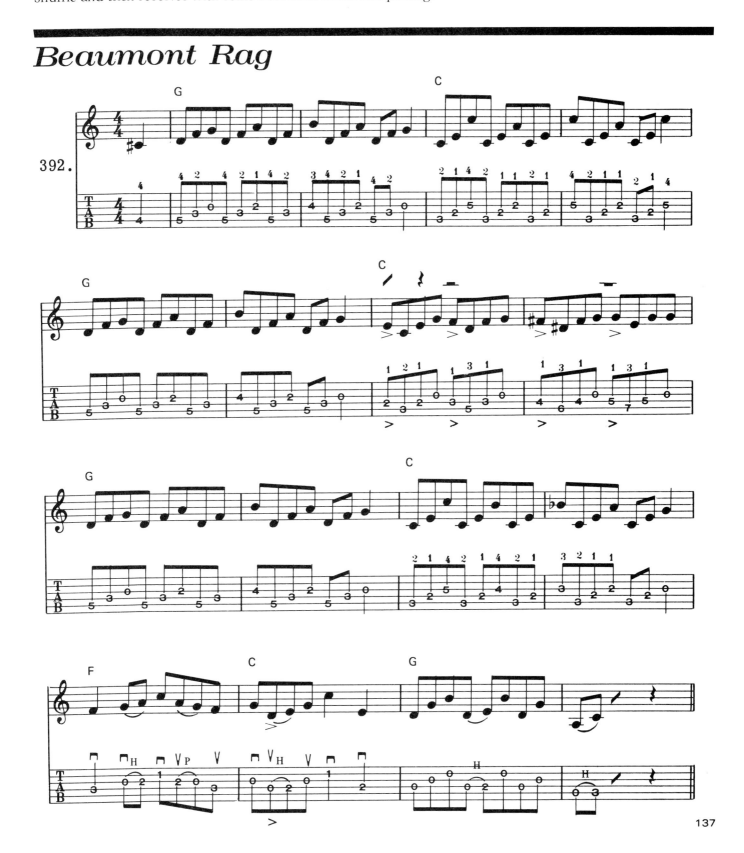

# Floating

Perhaps the most interesting technique to come under the modern crosspicking mantle is playing melodic lines by combining open strings and higher-position fingerings on neighboring strings. Dubbed *floating* (a name I'm not wild about, but nothing else has surfaced), this technique is simply a sustain-rich alternative to regular linear playing. But, with its emphasis on movement between strings and its tendency to roll down across three strings at regular intervals, it clearly qualifies as a crosspicking hybrid.

Here is how the A-part of "Dixie Hoedown" appears when played straight and then when floated.

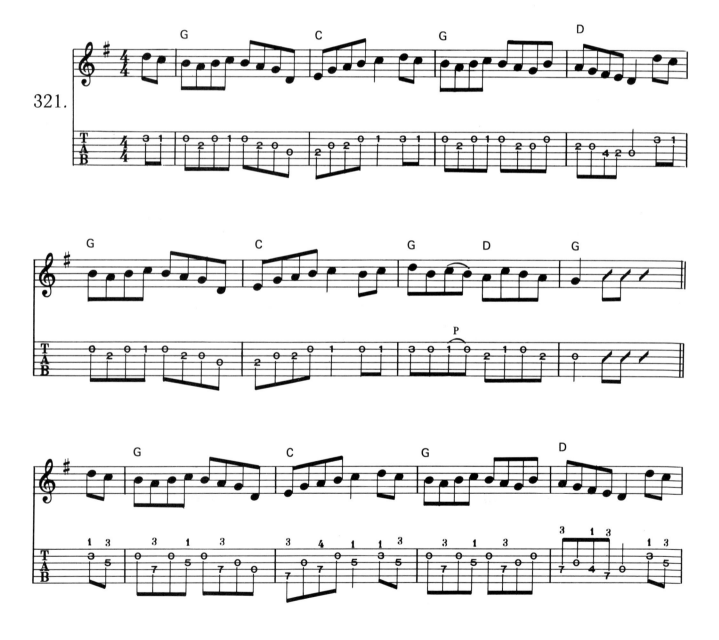

321.

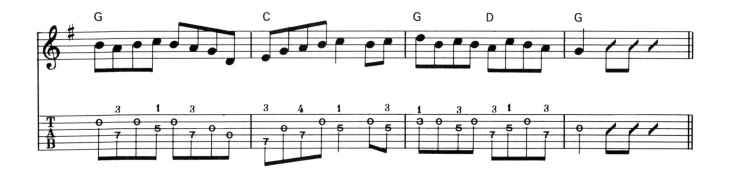

Like standard crosspicking (in fact like all special moves), floating is easily integrated into regular linear playing in whatever proportions you decide.

The momentary:

322.

The egalitarian:

323.

The totalitarian:

324.

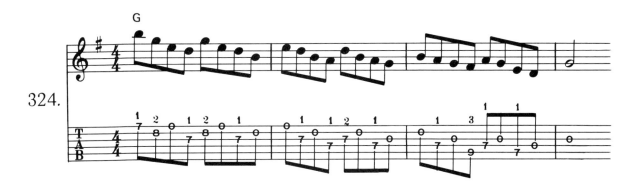

A couple of I V phrases now. Tony Rice played the first half of this first one in "Old Home Place."

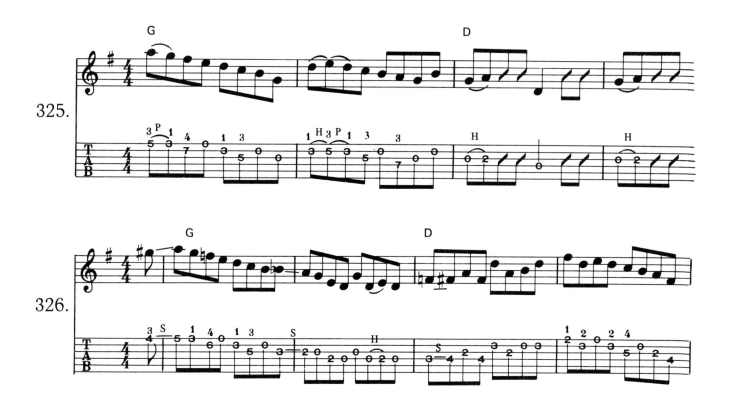

325.

326.

Two additional V measures:

327.

328.

Some I V I ending phrases:

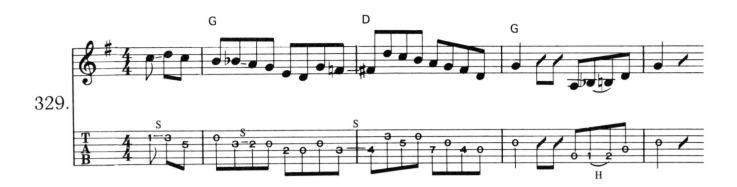

329.

This superb specimen is from Billy Henry, one of the top players in the Northeast.

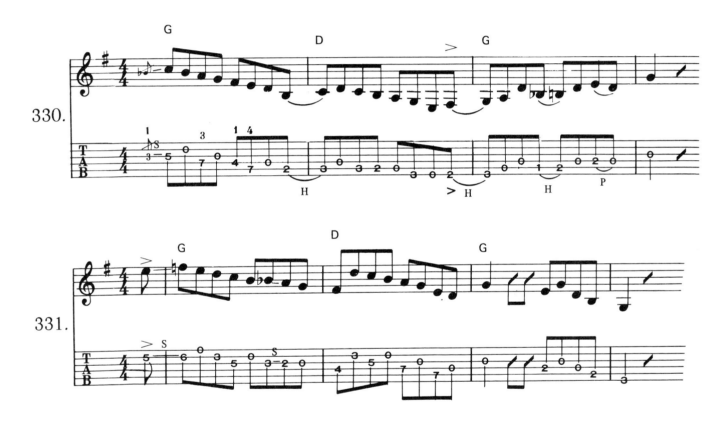

330.

331.

A couple of V I ending phrases in C:

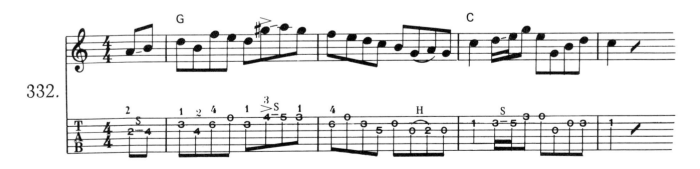

332.

333.

And a little higher-up C action with the floatatious ending I used on my recording of "Chicken Reel."

334.

As you can see, certain note/string combinations keep appearing in these examples regardless of the particular chord at hand. This repetition is not coincidental or the result of a parochial set of examples. Instead, it follows from the nature of floating itself; all told there is a relatively small number of moves available, and so the more common among them are pivotal.

For my floating last will and testament, here's a solo to "Rollin' in My Sweet Baby's Arms" that contains more of it than you're ever likely to hear in a single break but which works nonetheless; complete with trail-off.

Billy Henry

142

# Rollin' in My Sweet Baby's Arms

**396.**

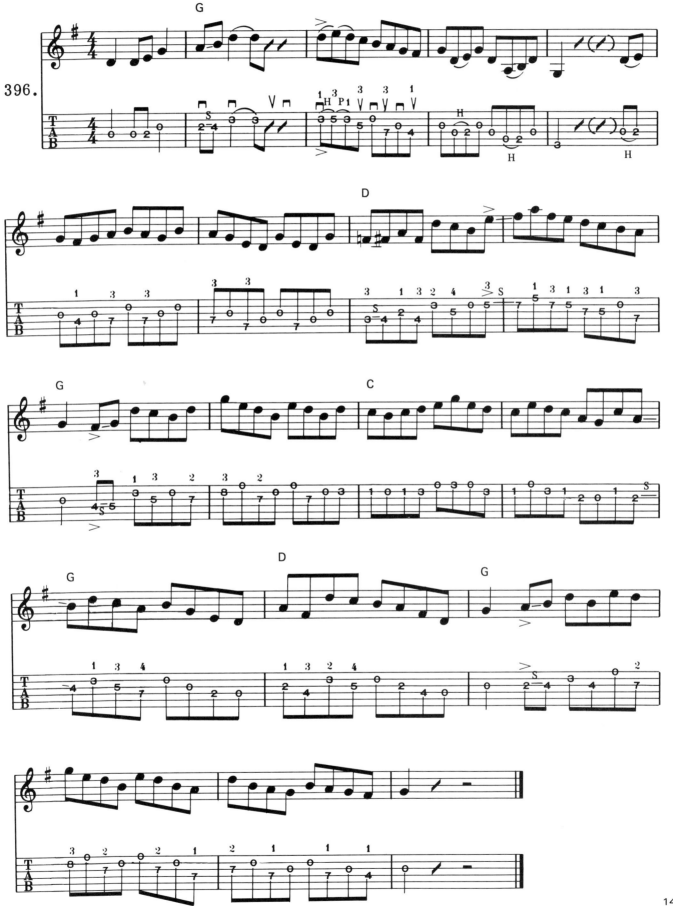

# Double-Stop Picking and Other Melodic-Motion Licks

All sorts of simple yet pleasing double-stop scales and other melodic-motion techniques exist within the network of fingerboard positions. Treated flexibly and combined with picking patterns that elaborate them, these motions can seed a vast inventory of pure licks, many of which are quite hot.

## Double-Stops

Here is a two-octave double-stop scale in C that features the first two strings.

335.

Notice that only two different positions are used throughout: the fingers are either one or two frets apart. These are the key double-stop patterns on adjacent strings.

This popular segment of the scale is a choice place to frame licks.

336.

Modifying it slightly we have a nice end-of-chorus riff.

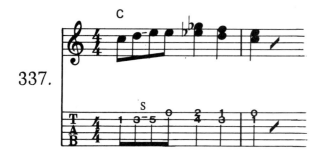

337.

Picking the double-stops in strictly linear fashion, and varying their order, we get an assortment of measure-long licks.

338.

339.

340.

Union Grove, 1973

Let's put some of these moves to use now in a solo.

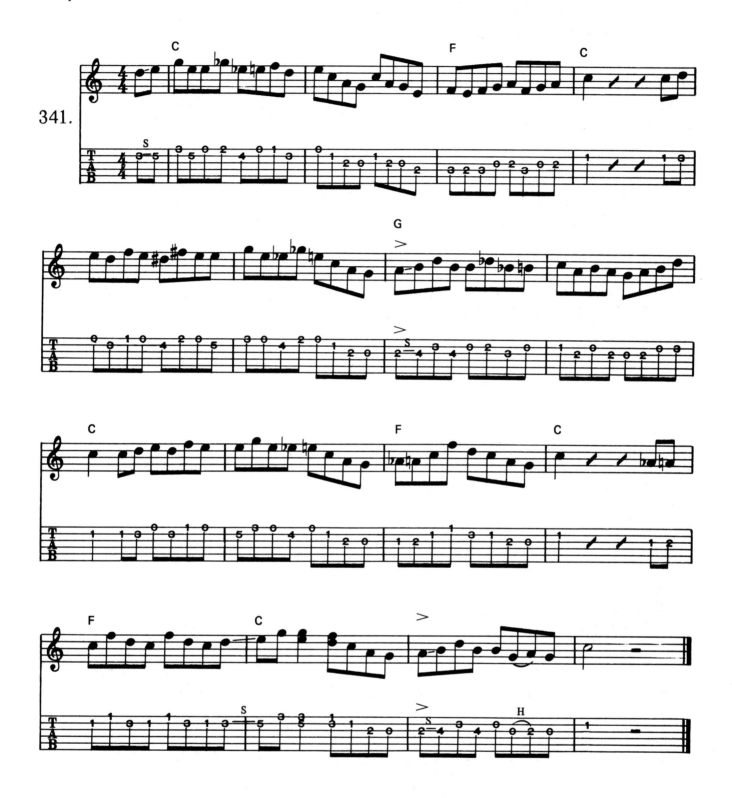

341.

This is just a start; the popular motion from which all of these licks sprang
occurs all over the fingerboard, and the same basic picking approaches apply.
Two frets up from where we started, for example, is the key of D.

**342.**

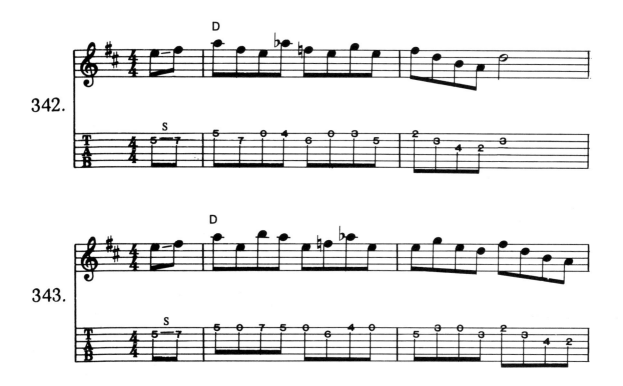

**343.**

Further up is G.

**344.**

**345.**

Yes—there is something cavalier about this approach to picking. Since the lick moves and the open strings do not, the open strings are often, in effect, random notes incorporated into an otherwise logical series. Would you believe it usually doesn't make much difference? The input of open strings in typical double-stop licks is still small enough that, except for those rare intolerable combinations (which you soon learn to avoid or modify), the basic sound carries. The great thing about licks like these is that if you play them with a straight face, your friends will think that you actually chose every note and maybe even that you know jazz.

Over on the bass end, here are some I IV V leads based on one basic set of double-stop motions. Each example is prefaced by a sketch of the particular double-stop motions involved.

**349.**

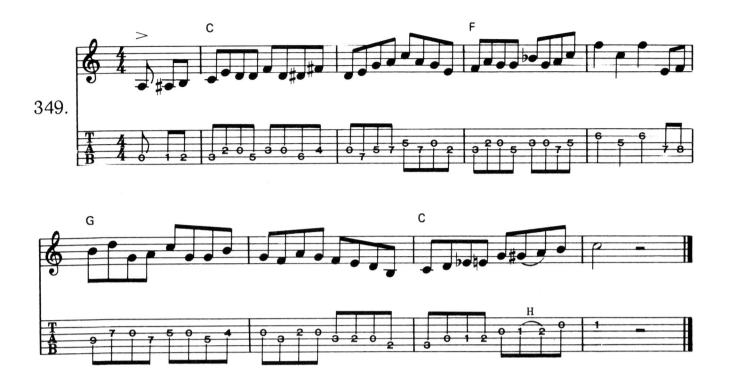

As with every kind of flatpicking, double-stop picking must be adapted as the situation demands; the ear muscles cannot remain idle. Here, planted in two popular locations, are the key double-stop patterns on nonadjacent strings.

**350.**

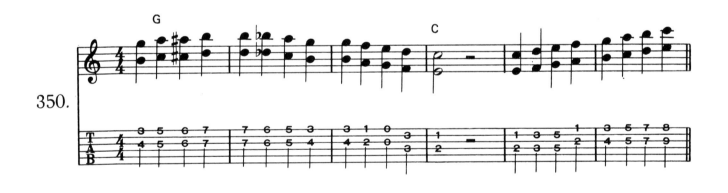

**351.**

And now the licks:

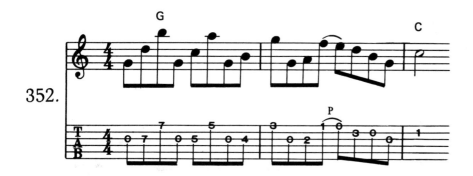

352.

Double-stop picking often resembles floating and the two naturally complement each other.

353.

Some of the sweetest licks going are those in which various double-stops are held and picked so that they ring without pause. Here are two.

354.

355.

Licks like these work well behind vocals during certain songs, and it's nice to occasionally punctuate your rhythm playing with them.

Now a little dancing I IV V I operation in G. Pay special attention to the way the D measure is picked; we could have simply followed the pattern we started with and used only the E as our open string but we chose something more demanding and interesting instead.

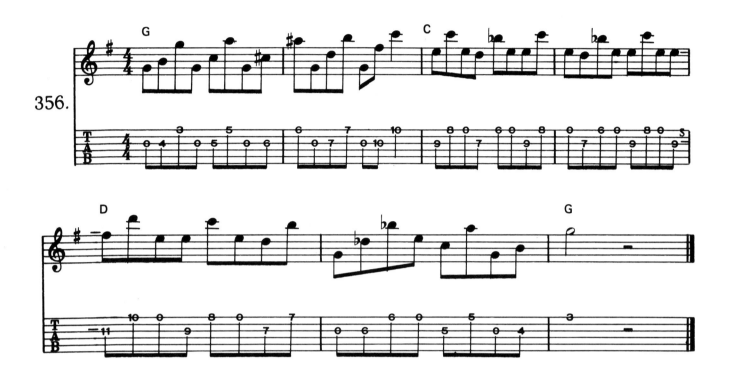

356.

Concentrating on the D chord now, we seek further intricacies with a group of D-to-G licks.

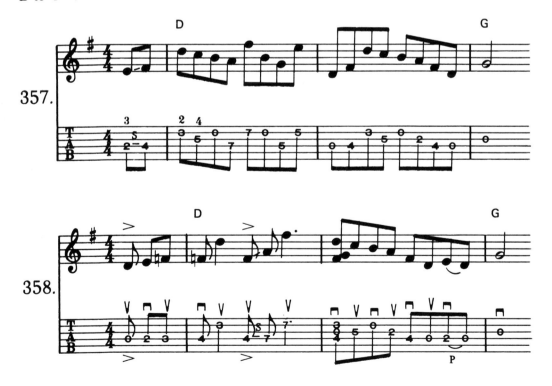

357.

358.

Highly intricate, if not baroque, and one of my favorites:

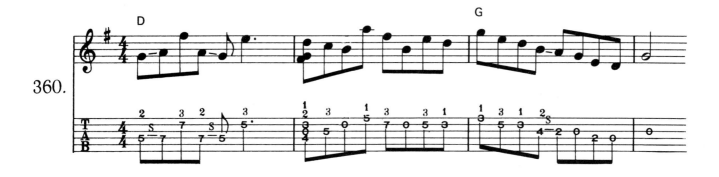

Moving down into the bass zone now, some of the richest-sounding combinations are called into play.

Dan Crary used this motif nicely in "Across the Big Sandy."

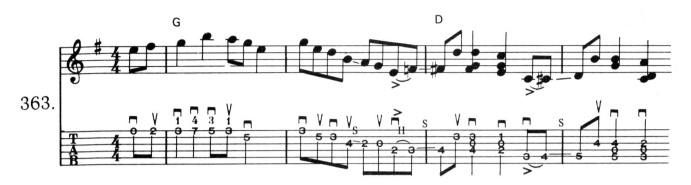

363.

Another of the ten I'd take with me to a desert island:

364.

And a higher jazzier variation to close:

365.

As you can see, combining simple melodic motions with convenient picking patterns is a remarkably fertile source of licks. Given a little tinkering, almost any motion you can think of can be translated into a lick. We'll finish our look at special effects now with some examples of high-level tinkering.

## Other Melodic-Motion Licks

Why-bother-with-different-fingerings motions are one important kind. Here are three that move from G to C.

366.

This one is from Mark O'Connor.

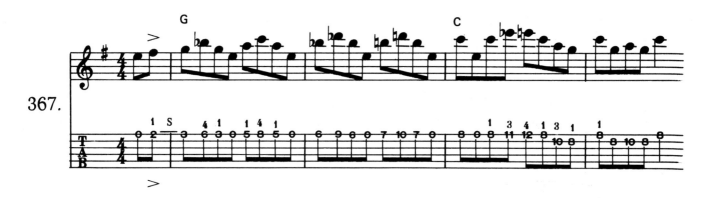

367.

This one I tailored for "Beaumont Rag."

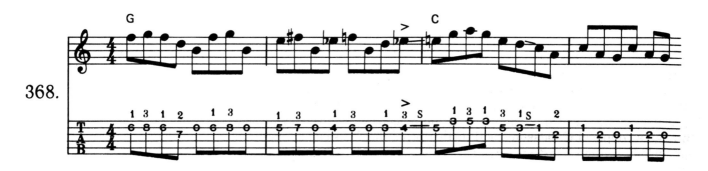

368.

Speaking of "Beaumont Rag," Clarence White liked to use this crosspicking-on-two-strings move for the stop.

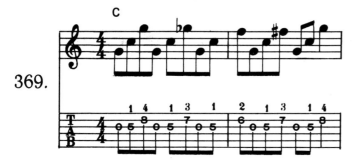

369.

Django Reinhardt was also fond of such moves. In G it goes:

Which brings us to this favorite Norman Blake move.

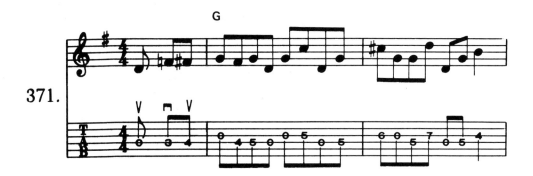

Norman Blake has also introduced a triple-stop series based on diminished sounds that's become one of the punchiest moves in flatpicking. Though your first response to this series might be "Oh no—they've finally landed," further reflection should yield the truth: It is an outrageously creative way to play through a couple of G measures and further proof that licks can spring from any melodic motion you devise. Starting with a little syncopated double-stop action in D:

Mark O'Connor—as he is prone to do—takes the concept one step further in
this artful elaboration (framed on a I V phrase).

And we'll take the concept and the chapter out now with these two endings.

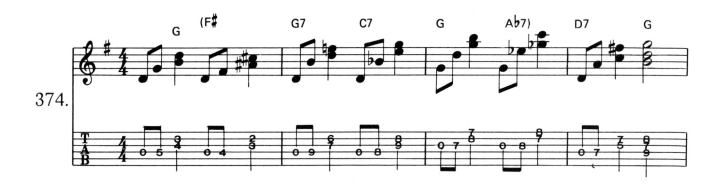

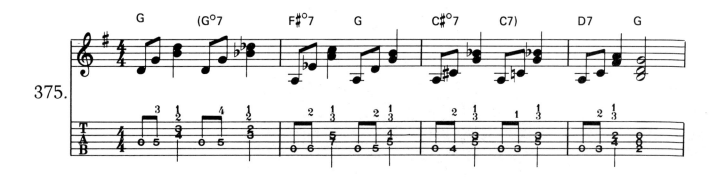

# Celebrity Section

For our last licks we turn to five of the most influential flatpickers in recorded history: Doc Watson, Dan Crary, Norman Blake, Tony Rice, and Mark O'Connor.

These master players have not only inspired and challenged all of us who flatpick, but they have also left their marks on the actual sound of the style. Flatpicking is young and still developing; it is a growing landscape of particular sounds as much as it is a physical technique. And the sounds of these five have become important features of that landscape.

# Doc Watson

Even if he hadn't been the original idol of most flatpickers and the one to make flatpicking a household word in the folk world, Doc Watson would still hold a very special place in our hearts. For his country soul, and the impeccable musical vision that flows from it, are irresistible; his singing and playing shine with an authenticity, economy, and warmth that is hard to beat. He is a gem.

Doc tours widely and records often. For the past couple years he has worked mostly in a trio with his son Merle on guitar and Michael Coleman on bass.

In keeping with the directness of his approach to melodies Doc treats licks more as a garnish than as a meal and he uses them sparingly. His specialty is the fine art of injecting licks into pauses while he's singing. Here are two versions of his favorite pause-in-the-middle lick, from his classic numbers "Way Downtown" and "Streamline Cannonball."

376.

377.

Both songs also feature striking pause-at-the-end licks. "Way Downtown":

378.

"Streamline Cannonball":

379.

The singing resumes in this one *before* the lick is over. Tricky.

Here is a beautiful G lick that Doc used as a pause-in-the-middle lick behind another singer in an early recording of "Crawdad," but which also (as you'll see next) works nicely in a standard ending phrase.

380.

Finally, here is the second half of a "New River Train" solo which features variations of some of the above licks and the economy version of the basic crosspicking shuffle.

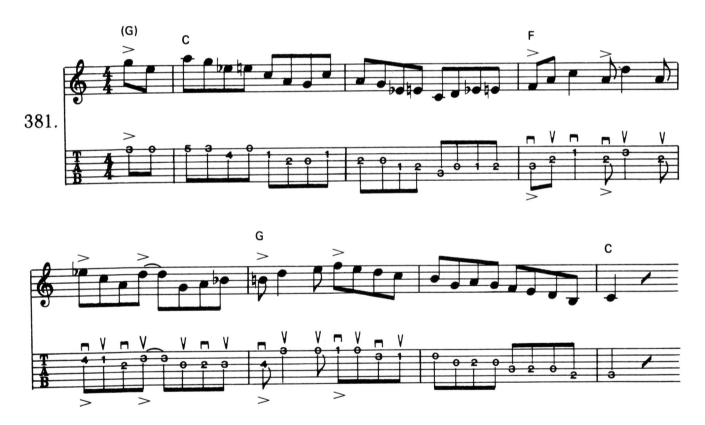

381.

# Dan Crary

Dan's place in the flatpicking pantheon was formally secured in 1972 with the release of his *Bluegrass Guitar* album on American Heritage Records. The first all-instrumental album to showcase flatpicking, it was an instant hit; powerful and interesting renditions of fiddle tunes which included frequent and effortless excursions up the neck (something we take for granted today but which was rare at the time).

Subsequent albums have enhanced Dan's reputation as a major player and as one who especially shines in the area of dynamics, i.e. coaxing different sounds and textures from the guitar in order to suit different songs. He is the flatpicking columnist for *Frets* magazine, sometimes tours as a solo performer, and is often seen with Berline, Crary, and Hickman.

Dan used this lead as an introduction to "Grey Eagle." We can use it to introduce him.

This blues solo (created for "Foggy Mountain Special") shows off two of Dan's specialties: working around an E chord and shifting a formulaic lick into fifth gear by adding triplets to it. My favorite is the lick which appears at the top of the fourth measure and then again at the top of the sixth—the E equivalent of Clarence White's G run. (Notice how it sounds slightly different in each location.)

This "Blackberry Blossom" B-part has everything. It begins with a normal first measure ("The ball is snapped, good protection from the defense"); slides into a stunning blues lick up the neck in the second ("Quarterback connects with the setback way downfield who then *laterals* to the wide receiver"); uses a formula lick around an A-minor bar at the seventh fret in the third ("Time out, there is a player down"); and then resolves with a lick which combines open strings and high positions and which moves so nicely that you're not aware you've just covered three chords with it ("Touchdown!").

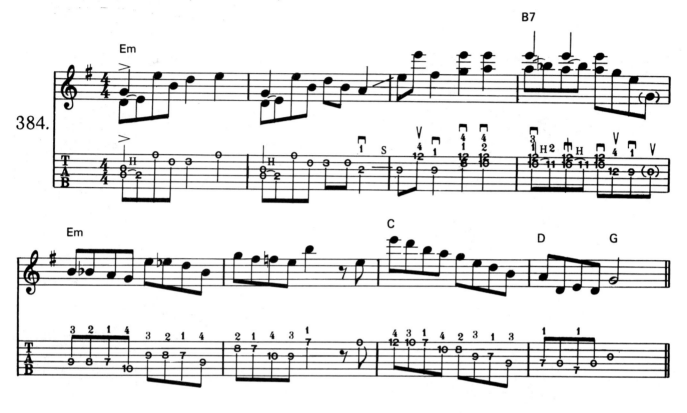

# Norman Blake

Combine a penchant for solo performing, a complex yet down-home approach to music, some southern soul, and a lot of luck and you may get Norman Blake, perhaps the most interesting stylist to come down the flatpicking pike.

Drive is the most obvious thing that sets Blake apart: In addition to normal linear picking his playing features a kind of hyperspaced Carter-style picking in which strums, double-stops, and bursts of crosspicking mingle with the melody to produce stunning, rhythm-charged leads. This rhythmic style has expanded our notions of what a single guitar is capable of and it stands out as Blake's special contribution (not to mention his choice of notes, which stands out even when he's picking normally).

Today Norman performs with the Rising Fawn Ensemble, a trio that includes his wife Nancy, and is also recognized as a gifted songwriter as well as a superb musician.

A practical lick with some of Norman's favorite pulloffs in the third measure:

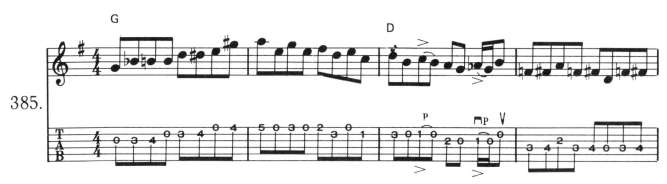

The exotic G lick here (in captivity for the first time ever) requires you to jump from the top of the neck to the bottom on short notice but provides a couple of open E notes to help.

386.

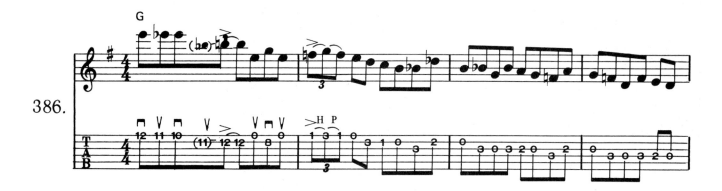

A gorgeous ending phrase. Strums and double-stops add a dimension to any lead they touch.

387.

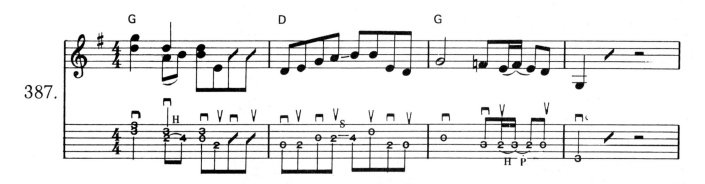

The magic-rhythm machine in all its glory. The line between strumming and picking often disappears when Blake is holding court (which can make capturing it on paper all the more ambitious).

388.

# Tony Rice

"And the winner in the bionic chops category is . . ."

Tony Rice is the embodiment of hot flatpicking. Emerging nationally in the mid seventies as guitarist with J.D. Crowe he was generally accepted as the musical heir of the late Clarence White (whose vintage Martin he plays). Tony scaled new heights of technique and became the leading agent of progressive bluegrass on the guitar. From there it was only a small step to Dawg music, which he helped pioneer in the original David Grisman ensemble and has continued to develop with his own Tony Rice Unit. But Tony has kept one foot firmly in bluegrass (as the Bluegrass Album Band's albums bear witness) and for this we are thankful for he is a remarkable singer and a peerless rhythm guitarist.

Tony's sound is taut and sleek and driving. He is a lick-oriented player, and the wardrobe of bluesy licks with which he attires his bluegrass solos is stunning; most players my age and younger have found ourselves thoroughly intoxicated by them.

This string of almost pure licks is from a solo Tony recorded for "Blue Ridge Mountain Home." It moves along fairly straightforwardly until the D measures at which point the slide on the A string inaugurates one of his favorite D licks (the first D measure), followed by a battery of pulloffs (the second D measure), followed by the omnipresent Clarence White G run.

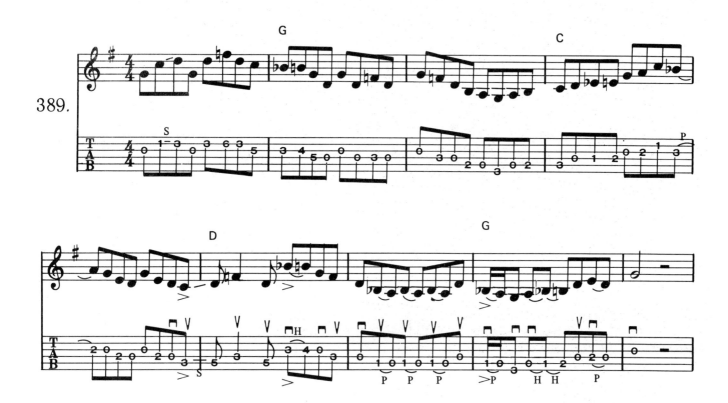

Now, one of the most potent jaw-droppers known to bluegrass man—the D lick Tony uses at the end of "You Don't Know My Mind." The challenge of this lick is the timing. Specifically, you need to play triplets (a) in succession, (b) without the aid of hammers and pulls (except for one), (c) with an accent on the first note of each. (Hint: You're going to wish you *had* let your right hand enroll in that Nautilus program when the special introductory offer appeared several weeks ago.)

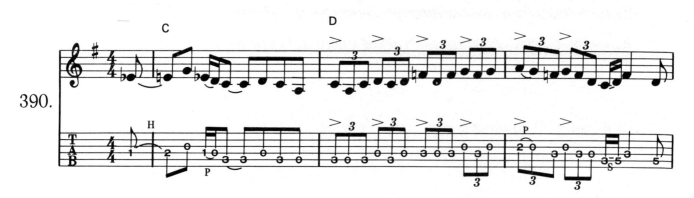

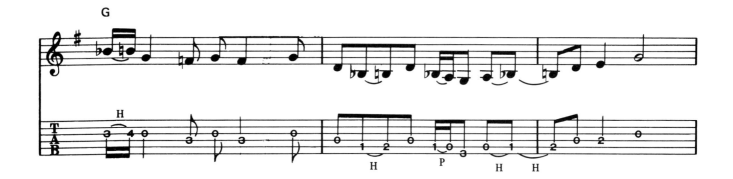

A classy, bluesy lead for the other popular ending phrase (courtesy of "Nine Pound Hammer").

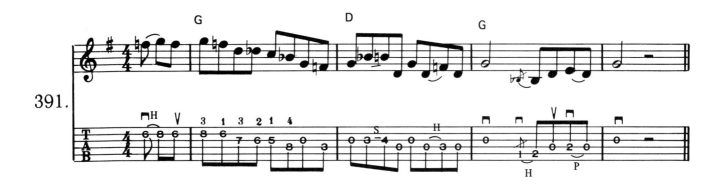

391.

If I was mayor of a town I would propose a holiday in honor of this lick. Tony used it in "On and On" but it works anywhere. I especially like the way it returns to the final G; a refreshing change from the usual G runs.

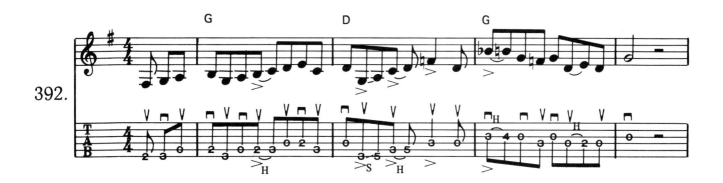

392.

# Mark O'Connor

Mark has those of us who swim the musical rivers wondering where he got the hydrofoil. While in junior high school he began blazing a trail of contest victories that is unlikely to be matched; in 1975, when he was 14, Mark won both the Grand Masters Fiddle Championship (fiddling was his first passion) and the National Flatpicking Championship. In recent years his talents have propelled him into the David Grisman Quintet, the Dregs, and (coming full circle) some touring and recording with Doc Watson. Today, at 23, he's a free agent and living in Nashville.

Mark's flatpicking is dazzling. Like his fiddling, it is lyrical and fluid and melodic like nobody's business and it is underwritten by awesome technique; he can do whatever he wants to. If his explosive creativity led to occasional excesses early on (and, hey, how many fully developed twelve-year-old recording artists do *you* know?), it has also led to enough musical peaks to last you or I more than a lifetime. Flatpicking is fortunate that the guitar joined the fiddle in Mark's priorities.

Mark's two recordings of "Dixie Breakdown" are virtual encyclopedias of hot licks, as the three following excerpts make plain. It is fascinating to hear how Mark has imbibed and expanded on the sounds of the stylists that came before him. For example, you can tell from the way this first excerpt opens that Tony Rice is no stranger here. But neither is he a static presence: O'Connor the alchemist has been at play.

393.

Try finding a more beautiful bluesy lick than the one that opens this passage.

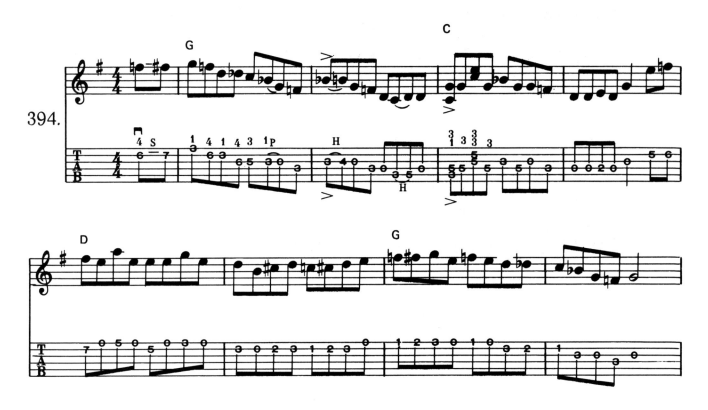

394.

And an ending of substance (with some diminished-run action in the third and fourth measures):

395.

# Select Discography

The number of albums featuring flatpicking has grown from a trickle to a stream in recent years. While this has effectively eliminated eighth-note deficiency in the industrialized world, it has also presented prospective record buyers with more choices than ever before. To help, here are one or two suggested albums from each of the major stylists. Obviously many fine recordings—both by these artists and by others—go unmentioned in such a listing; it's a starter kit, not a survey.

**Doc Watson**
*Live on Stage*
Vanguard VSD 9/10

This two-record set was *the* ear-opener for many of us. Listen to "Salt Creek" and "Billy in the Lowground."

*Southbound*
Vanguard VRS 9170

Smooth and hot. Contains "Nashville Pickin'" and the classic "Nothin' to It."

**Dan Crary**
*Bluegrass Guitar*
American Heritage 275

A classic. The first all-instrumental flatpicking LP. Great up-the-neck activity.

*Guitar*
Sugar Hill 3730

Dan's most recent, an impeccable modern production with hot young sidemen.

**Norman Blake**
*Live at McCabes*
Tacoma D-1052

Live and largely solo.

*Whiskey Before Breakfast*
Rounder 0063

Norman's "guitar" album. A very satisfying and consistent effort.

**Tony Rice**
*Guitar*
King KB29

Early Tony, featuring some solid bluegrass with J.D. and crew.

*Manzanita*
Rounder 0092

More than a flatpicking record—a total listening experience.

**Mark O'Connor**
*Pickin' in the Wind*
Rounder 0068

With the outrageous live "Dixie Breakdown."

*Markology*
Rounder 0090

Mark's "guitar" album. With the outrageous studio "Dixie Breakdown."

**Clarence White**
*The Kentucky Colonels:*
*"Appalachian Swing"*
Liberty 10185

The only studio album to feature this late master on the acoustic guitar. A recent budget reissue of a United Artists release.

And, might we add . . .

**Orrin Star**
*No Frets Barred*                          A must for any collection.
Flying Fish 267

**Orrin Star and Gary Mehalick**
*Premium Blend*                            How do they do it?
Flying Fish 234

All of the above records are available from the following mail-order houses:

County Sales            Roundup Records
Box 191                 P.O. Box 154
Floyd, VA 24091         North Cambridge, MA 02140

## About the Author

Orrin Star is a Boston based bluegrass and folk musician recognized for his virtuoso guitar, banjo, and mandolin playing as well as for his wry sense of humor. In 1976 he won the National Flatpicking Championship (the largest bluegrass guitar contest in the country). He also formed a duo with Gary Mehalick that came to be highly regarded in acoustic-music circles. In recent months he's been appearing as a solo performer and writing for *Mandolin World News.* He has performed throughout the United States and Europe and has two albums on Flying Fish Records.

For those of you who have a hard time learning music from the printed page, I have recorded a cassette of all the licks in the book that do not appear on the soundsheet. This tape also features some additional spoken comments on certain of the licks and is available from: HOMESPUN TAPES
Box 694
Woodstock, NY 12498